TRIBUTES
BY FRIENDS
OF DAVID PAWSON

TRIBUTES
BY FRIENDS
OF DAVID PAWSON

Edited by Kim Tan

Anchor Recordings

Copyright © 2020 David Pawson Ministry CIO

The right of David Pawson to be identified as author of this Work has been asserted by him in accordance with the Copyright, Designs and Patents Act 1988.

First published in Great Britain in 2020 by
Anchor Recordings Ltd
Synegis House, 21 Crockhamwell Road,
Woodley, Reading RG5 3LE

No part of this publication may be reproduced or transmitted in any form or by any means, electronic or mechanical, including photocopy, recording or any information storage and retrieval system, without prior permission in writing from the publisher.

For more of David Pawson's teaching, including DVDs and CDs, go to www.davidpawson.com

FOR FREE DOWNLOADS
www.davidpawson.org

For further information,
email: info@davidpawsonministry.com

ISBN 978-1-913472-21-4

Printed by Ingram Spark

CONTENTS

	Introduction	9
1.	Message from the Trustees of the David Pawson Teaching Trust	11
2.	David Pawson Tribute at Millmead Church by Dr Kim Tan on 21 May 2020.	13
3.	David Pawson: The Millmead Legacy *Tribute by Dr Ian Stackhouse (UK)*	17
4.	David Pawson: An Anglican Evangelical? *Tribute by Rev Canon Clive Hawkins (UK)*	23
5.	David Pawson: Among the Churches in Borneo *Tribute by Dr Thomas Chung (Malaysia)*	29
6.	David Pawson: His Online Ministry *Tribute by Steve Dally (UK)*	33
7.	David Pawson: Friend of Opwekking Ministries *Tribute by Henk Dik (Netherlands)*	39
8.	David Pawson: One of the Greatest Bible Teachers of his Generation *Tribute by Sam Hailes (UK)*	43
9.	David Pawson: Preaching to the Whole World *Tribute by Jim Harris (UK)*	49
10.	David Pawson: Man of God *Tribute by Malcolm Hedding (Israel)*	53
11.	David Pawson: A Gentle and Generous Spiritual Giant *Tribute by Dr Daniel Ho (Malaysia)*	59
12.	David Pawson: Brilliant and Complex *Tribute by Dr Philip Lyn (Malaysia)*	67

13. David Pawson: Bible Teacher Extraordinaire *Tribute by Philip Pillai (Singapore)*	73
14. David Pawson: A Friend of International Children's Leader and Punk Rocker *Tribute by Revd Ian Smale (aka Ishmael) (UK)*	79
15. David Pawson: Mentor via Phone *Tribute by John Spall (Australia)*	83
16. David Pawson: An Elderly English Gentleman *Tribute by Steve and Elaine Spillman (USA)*	87
17. David Pawson: Teacher of the Chinese Church *Tribute by Tony Tseng (Taiwan)*	91
18. David Pawson: De-Greecing the Church *Tribute by Peter Tsukahira (Israel)*	95
19. David Pawson: An Appreciation *Tribute by Mike Wakely (Pakistan)*	99
20. David Pawson: A Critic of Prosperity Teaching *Tribute by Kenny Wirya (Indonesia)*	105
21. David Pawson: In Democratic Republic of Congo *Tribute by Dr Philip Wood (DR Congo)*	109
22. David Pawson: A Spiritual Father *Tribute by Tan Sri Sir Francis Yeoh (Malaysia)*	113
23. David Pawson: Scholar & Communicator *Tribute by Dr Kim Tan (UK)*	117
24. David Pawson: Other Tributes	123
George Verwer (UK)	123
Yang Tuck Yoong (Singapore)	123
Lesley Conder (UK)	125
Dan Murphy (Australia)	126
Postscript	127

INTRODUCTION
JOHN DAVID PAWSON
FEBRUARY 1930 – MAY 2020

David Pawson passed away on the 21 May 2020, on Ascension Day. To many around the world, he was a teacher, pastor, mentor and friend. To his family, he was a husband, father and grandfather. To the members of Guildford Baptist Church, better known as Millmead, he is fondly remembered by his initials, "JDP". He will be missed.

This is a collection of tributes written by David's friends from around the world. It contains personal stories of their friendships with David as well as accounts of how David's teaching ministry has impacted them and others in the churches in their countries. Some have also reflected theologically on David's teachings and they have not been shy about their disagreements with David. But David never insisted that everyone should agree with him on everything in order to be a friend. On the contrary, he welcomed lively discussions, especially on subjects deemed "controversial" (a label often attached to David).

In these tributes, we see different aspects of David that are not as well known but that have endeared him to his friends. We begin with a message from the Trustees of the David Pawson Teaching Trust (posted on the website), followed by two tributes given at Millmead by me and the current pastor, Dr Ian Stackhouse. These are followed by a tribute from the Revd Canon Clive Hawkins, Rector at St Mary's Church in Basingstoke, which David and Enid attended for 35 years after David retired from Millmead. The rest of the contributions are in alphabetical order, ending with a postscript.

We have all been deeply impacted by David and we all wanted to pay our tributes, to say "Thank you, David for inspiring us with the Word, for your wise counsel, for your example as a servant leader, for your generosity and friendship. But also for your love of life, your hobbies – architecture, cars, and art – and for your humour with all the wonderful Jewish jokes."

1. MESSAGE FROM THE TRUSTEES OF THE DAVID PAWSON TEACHING TRUST

JOHN DAVID PAWSON, FEB 1930 – MAY 2020

DAVID ASCENDED TO BE WITH HIS LORD AND SAVIOUR AT 9AM ON ASCENSION DAY, 21 MAY 2020

I first met David some 35 years ago in Abingdon where he was trialling his *'Unlocking the Bible'* talks. Each week I would eagerly travel from Basingstoke to Abingdon hungry for the next episode. David heard that I was from his own home town and so we would occasionally travel in together.

The word used of David more than most seems to be "controversial" but David was never controversial for its own sake. He was hungry for the truth and appealed constantly for people to check the Bible themselves to see whether what he was saying was true.

In the years that followed, David and I became dear friends. We would spend hours together sat next to the pond in his back garden pondering life. Like others in this book, I knew a kind and thoughtful man, a man full of terrible jokes and a thousand stories. We would laugh together and occasionally cry together. We would talk about very personal matters, the passing of his daughter, Enid's care after his death and much more. Strangely, one morbid topic that we would return to on numerous occasions was whether, in old age, we would prefer to lose our bodily functions or our minds. Well, for David it was his body, yet he still managed to smile and laugh his way through the somewhat un-dignifying support he needed in his last days.

I remember travelling together with him to many of his engagements. On the return journey we would try to find a route that would take us past the Mill House Pub near Odiham. He really loved those barbecue ribs. Above all, I enjoyed our travels through Israel together. So many rich memories and learnings.

David asked me to act as Chair of the David Pawson Teaching Trust in the early 2000s. The Trust was the idea of my good friend Kim Tan and was purposed to protect and promote David's teaching after his days. That day is now upon us.

In some ways, David was a bit of an enigma. A magnificent orator in front of thousands but socially awkward in groups of two or three. Yet his legacy is huge, with many thousands finding the Lord through his ministry. He leaves us with a wealth of biblical recorded wisdom. He was passionate about teaching the truth and exposing error and, specifically, encouraging everyone to read the Bible for themselves.

Our thoughts and prayers are with David's wife Enid and family at this time of great loss and we are also grateful to the staff at Oak Lodge Nursing Home who have shown David an amazing amount of care and love over the past twelve months.

Due to the current lockdown situation in the UK, the funeral service, held on 2 June was a private family matter, but we do hope to organise a thanksgiving and celebration service later this year or at a time when lockdown is lifted and more people can come and celebrate David's life.

David struggled with cancer of the bones and Parkinson's Disease symptoms for many years, which caused a gradual and progressive deterioration of his body. We thank the Lord that he was not impacted by the Coronavirus.

His ministry continues.

DAVE REBBETTES
CHAIRMAN, DAVID PAWSON TEACHING TRUST

2. DAVID PAWSON TRIBUTE AT MILLMEAD CHURCH BY KIM TAN ON 21 MAY 2020

AS THE UK WAS IN A LOCKDOWN DUE TO THE COVID 19 PANDEMIC, THIS WAS PRE-RECORDED FOR THE SERVICE WHICH WAS LIVE STREAMED. WWW.DAVIDPAWSON.COM/TRIBUTE_KT

My name is Kim Tan, one of the founding trustees of the David Pawson Teaching Trust. I am delighted to be asked to pay a tribute to David Pawson who sadly passed away on Thursday 21 May on Ascension Day. How appropriate that David should go to be with his Lord on Ascension Day, a subject he loved preaching on.

David was considered by many to be one of the finest bible expositors we've ever had. I came to study at the university of Surrey because I was told there was a very good Bible teacher at Millmead Church in Guildford. For five wonderful years, I, along with 1,500 other members, sat under his expository teaching.

David was at Millmead for about 14 years (1968–1981). It was here at Millmead that the foundation of his future ministry was laid. Twice on Sunday, he would teach, usually a series through one of the books of the Bible. This was recorded on cassette tapes, which were initially meant to be distributed to the elderly or those ill at home. No Zoom or live stream those days. Those tapes, however, then went worldwide to pastors and missionaries. I was told that even Billy Graham was a subscriber at one stage. Some even ended up in the jungles of Borneo. Imagine my surprise when taking a church camp and visiting an Iban longhouse (former head-hunters) and finding David's cassette tapes there.

The Trust have taken the Millmead tapes, digitised them and made them available for free through the David Pawson website. Today, there are over 1,700 teaching audios. His 300 teaching videos have been viewed 21 million times since 2011. This does not include the daily satellite broadcast into China in Mandarin.

In addition to that, the audio tapes from Millmead have been transcribed into book commentaries [like the *Come with me through* series]. There are now over 80 titles with many translated into six languages (Spanish, Mandarin, German, Indonesian, Russian and Portuguese).

The videos, audios and books constitute David's remarkable and enduring legacy to the Church.

From my perspective, no one has had more impact on the growth of the church in Southeast Asia in the past 30 years than David. Many of the leaders of the churches today have been impacted by David through his video and audio ministry.

But for me, David's greatest legacy will be his series on *Unlocking the Bible* – a series introducing the background and main themes of each book of the Bible. This was recorded over 90 hours and is available in video, audio and book format. Go buy a copy. Or watch the videos. It will inspire you to study the Bible for yourselves.

Two final reflections. One aspect of David that deeply impacted me was his integrity and humility. He didn't seek fame or fortune. And I have many stories from my travels with him. But just this one story here. I had a hard time persuading David to set up a trust to promote his teaching. The reason was that he did not want to build an organisation. He had no secretary, PA or manager; he had no laptop, email account, smartphone or iPad, although one of the trustees did try to persuade David to use one so he could watch Downton Abbey on it! He always wrote with pen and paper in longhand. He finally agreed after two years of persuasion to set up the Trust on condition that I promised that we would not send out letters asking for donations, that he would not benefit financially and that his teachings would be free for everyone. The trustees have kept the promise so that even in his death, David will continue to bless millions around the world for many years to come.

The other reflection is that David set a very high standard for many of us Bible teachers. He was meticulous in his preparation (he told me it takes him a year to prepare for a series), a perfectionist, an avid reader and scribbler of books with his red pen and had an amazing gift of communication – he took difficult ideas and made them simple to understand in his calm manner. With David, there was no performance or shouting or theatrics when he taught. He didn't want to attract attention to himself but instead wanted to "just let the Word speak". Just his calm, soothing manner with the occasional Geordie accent - that became his trademark. In his teaching, he touched both the head as well as the heart.

We remember at this time especially Enid his wife, confidant and, according to David, his biggest fan as well as biggest critic, and his son, Richard and daughter, Angela, and their families. They have sacrificed immensely to enable David's ministry to have such a huge global impact. I hope they will be comforted by the knowledge of how much David was loved and the millions of lives that have been impacted by him.

His was truly a life well lived. I have no doubt whatsoever that he was welcomed home with the words from his Lord, "Well done, good and faithful servant."

3. DAVID PAWSON: THE MILLMEAD LEGACY
TRIBUTE BY DR IAN STACKHOUSE

Ian Stackhouse became the Senior Pastor of Millmead in 2004 and has been in ministry for over thirty years. He is a pastor-theologian, a regular speaker at conferences and a part-time lecturer at London School of Theology. Ian has authored four books, including the Gospel Driven Church, which was based on his PhD thesis.

If I had a pound for every time someone asked me over the years whether I am the pastor of David Pawson's church, I would be a wealthy man by now. Almost every few months, even now after such a long time, someone will turn up hoping to be shown round the church where David Pawson preached, and, on one or two occasions, even hoping that they might see him.

As a matter of fact, Millmead is not David Pawson's church. It is an appellation he would have been very uncomfortable with. The church belongs to Jesus Christ. And besides, there have been two pastoral leaders between David and myself, both of whom had very distinguished ministries (Bob Roxburgh [1982–1989]; Peter Nodding [1990–2000]). Nevertheless, I am sure both Bob and Peter would agree with me that there was something very special about those Pawson years at Millmead. Most would say, in fact, that the ministry he exercised at that time, centred on his expository preaching of the Bible, was really what defined David, what made him so sought after around the world, and what I would like to focus on here, as we celebrate his life.

David arrived in Guildford in 1968, having had a very fruitful ministry at Gold Hill Baptist Church in Buckinghamshire. He was a visionary and led Guildford Baptist Church from its building in Commercial Road to the Millmead site. It was very much state of the art and became the epicentre of renewal during those next 14 years. At a time when the Bible was under growing attack from theological liberalism, as well as being side-lined, perhaps more insidiously by those on the extreme end of the charismatic renewal, David committed himself to teaching and preaching the whole counsel of God – including the bits that are hard to swallow. There were not many leaders who had the courage to do that, but David saw it as critical for the survival of evangelical Christianity. He believed the old adage that he who marries the spirit of this age will become a widower in the next. Although I was not around at that time – I was converted in 1981 – I know for a fact that his preaching was a lifeline for so many believers, not just the multitudes who beat a path to Millmead, but also the thousands more who subscribed to his tape ministry.

I am not alone in thinking that David flourished best when he was in situ in a congregation, and fully immersed in week-by-week expository preaching. He had an ability like no one else to go through the books of the Bible, bringing out the context and applying its truth. As a matter of fact, I once heard him at a preachers' conference unlocking (to use David's word) the Song of Songs. As a young preacher, trying to learn my craft, I was mesmerised by the way he exegeted the text. I couldn't believe what he got out of the passages. To have sat under this kind of ministry week after week must have been overwhelming for the congregation, as well as for David himself, as the one who was called to this task.

Once he left Millmead, however, I wonder whether he lost the grounding that this kind of settled ministry can give.

What he gained in terms of the freedom to itinerate – and what the world gained in an outstanding Bible teacher – he lost, I believe, in terms of pastoral rootedness. Indeed, my own opinion is that David started to make something of a virtue of his contrariness. I guess this is a danger for all who carry a prophetic mantle: the temptation to ruffle feathers just for the sake of it. On one occasion David admitted to me that when he went to a church with a Reformed theology, he would preach a sermon that had a bent towards an Arminian theology; and when he went to a church with an Arminian theology, he would preach a sermon that had a bent towards a Reformed theology. Although I understood the reasoning behind this, it struck me as just a little bit belligerent. Mind you, even if you disagreed with David, such was the hypnotic effect of his teaching that you would always come away from listening to him completely dazzled. David barely raised his voice, but he held complete attention; likewise, he barely moved his body, but you couldn't take your eyes off him. I have seen congregations literally enraptured as David held forth from the pulpit. All the more amazing, then, that David didn't seek the limelight. He could have done so ten times over. Instead, he set about his task with real humility.

One of the many things I admired about David was the way he stuck to his principles. Again, it didn't always make for a pleasant ride, but he was at least consistent. For example, David believed in the priesthood of all believers, so the idea that anyone might use the term "Reverend" was anathema to him. Everywhere he went he was either Mr Pawson, or just David Pawson. Not unrelated to this, he believed that the church is not a building but people. When I went to see him back in 2006, to inform him out of courtesy of our decision to remodel the Millmead Centre, he simply said: "It's just bricks and steel. You can do what you want with it." Cheekily, it is a quote I reminded him of as I showed him round the new Millmead Centre a couple of years ago. It is one thing to say something like that, but I could see that he was visibly shocked to see how radically we had changed things. I don't blame him. Millmead was in many ways his home. Nevertheless, he knew, as well as anyone, that unless you change things, a church can get locked in its past. So, I would like to think he approved, even if it was hard to bear emotionally.

Which brings me to another aspect of David that I would like to honour, and that is his warmth and kindness. For someone who could be very imposing in the pulpit, and not frightened to call things out, you would think he would be a bit unfriendly. But nothing could have been further from the truth. I know this first-hand, but I also know many others who were touched by David's generosity. My good friend Philip Greenslade, for example, a young minister in nearby Woking at the time, told me that it was David who helped him learn how to drive. I don't know why this particularly stands out for me. It doesn't sound particularly heroic. But when I think of how easy it is as a minister to hide behind books, or to think of oneself as above such ordinariness, the image of David just sitting in the passenger seat of a car, helping his friend towards passing his driving test, strikes me as most endearing. I spoke to Richard, his son, the evening of the day David passed away – Ascension Day, as it happens – and he told me of all the tricks his Dad used to play on the grandchildren. I can imagine it. David had a delightful sense of humour. He reminded me of my own father-in-law who would often say something shocking but with just a little twinkle in his eye.

It will be for others in this book to comment on David's writing, his audio ministry, and the phenomenal impact he has had more recently on the church in the Far East. I said to someone the other day: if I had just a fraction of the fruit that David enjoyed throughout his ministry, I would be very happy indeed. In fact, I am so in awe of the sheer scale of David's influence, I wouldn't even put myself in the same sentence as him. His has been a most remarkable ministry, and those years at Millmead, as I say, were truly astonishing. Notwithstanding the fact that tales get taller in the telling, I really do think the queues to hear David preach at Millmead extended to the A3 (the motorway into Guildford), or could have.

Inheriting the leadership of a church that has experienced such blessings in the past is not easy, as I am sure you can imagine. Add to that the conviction with which David held his views and you will appreciate that it has at times proved well-nigh impossible. I have observed over the years how hard it has been for some of his core followers to countenance theological views other than David's without feeling they were betraying his teaching, and indeed the gospel. Had we been tinkering with the deity of Christ, or the doctrine of the Atonement, I could have understood it. But we weren't. We were simply charting a different course on what theologians regard as disputable matters. But for David nothing was disputable. It was all very clear. Hence, the disapprobation if you disagreed with David. The certainties that he was renowned for, and which strengthened a generation, could also prove something of a barrier to real dialogue.

Even so, I'm not complaining. The reason Millmead has been an utter delight to do ministry in, and just about the most perfect pulpit for me to preach in, is in large part because of David Pawson. The actual pulpit has gone now. As I write, a certain Welshman called Stephen Owen is designing a new pulpit for the new auditorium. But the theatre remains, and the hunger for the Word endures. David left a legacy at Millmead of people who love the scriptures and who seek in every which way to embody them in their everyday lives.

In that sense, the genius of Millmead, as I heard David say on more than one occasion, is not its preaching, even when he was there, but the fact that it is a real live Christian community. Indeed, he told me once that the reason the auditorium is shaped as it is, like an amphitheatre, is because he wanted people to see the glory of God on each other's faces as they gathered together, Sunday by Sunday. Quirky, I know, but as someone who has preached in that space these past 16 years, he was right. It is not the pulpit that is the focus of the church, but the people.

I heard of David's passing just an hour or so before I was due to live-stream an Ascension Day service from the new chapel at Millmead. In terms of putting together a tribute, it was short notice indeed. On the other hand, I knew David well enough to know that the last thing he would have wanted was to turn this celebration of our Lord's ascension – a doctrine he felt passionate about – into a eulogy to himself. So apart from announcing his death, giving a few preliminary reflections, and offering prayers for the family, I carried on with what we had prepared, knowing full well that this was the best tribute I could pay him. He was, in the final analysis, a follower of Jesus Christ.

Having said that, I am deeply grateful for this opportunity now, to state more fully in writing my appreciation of David Pawson. Whether the angels in heaven will be ready for such a man, I don't know. I can't imagine they would have met too many people as passionate about truth as David, nor as gifted in communicating it. What I do know, however, as Kim Tan said himself in his own tribute on the Millmead live stream, is that David Pawson will have received, on entering his rest, a resounding "Well done, good and faithful servant."

4. DAVID PAWSON: AN ANGLICAN EVANGELICAL?

TRIBUTE BY REVD CANON CLIVE HAWKINS

The Revd Canon Clive Hawkins studied theology at St Peter's College, Oxford and trained for ordination at Trinity College, Bristol. He has at various times been an Area Dean, member of the Bishop's Council, the General Synod and the Crown Nominations Commission and a speaker at Spring Harvest and WORD Alive. He is the Rector of St Mary's Church, Eastrop Basingstoke, the church, for over thirty-five years, which David and Enid attended, ministered in occasionally but of which they were never members. He thought it might damage his credibility if it were erroneously thought he was now an Anglican evangelical!

I first came across David in the summer of 1976, when three friends and I were spending our last Sundays at University visiting some of the renowned churches of England. Millmead in Guildford, where David was the pastor, was one of them. Two others were in London at All Souls, Langham Place with John Stott and St Helen's Bishopsgate with Dick Lucas, and St Michael le Belfry in York with David Watson.

I recall that we had to rush out of the service to catch the train, which we did, but only just in my case. About half an hour later, when the guard came round asking to see our tickets I asked, "When's the train getting into Oxford?" The guard replied, "It isn't, it's going to Margate!"

David had an interested and enquiring mind. He loved looking into the details of things, which, combined with his ability to see the wood from the trees, made him a very clear Bible teacher. His reputation was truly worldwide. He wrote more than 75 books, produced more than 300 teaching videos and well over 1,500 audio recordings. It began with cassette tapes of his sermons and then moved on to videos, CDs, DVDs, and more recently through YouTube, where he has 61,000 subscribers. Some of these videos have attracted well over 250,000 viewers and he is regularly watched and listened to in 120 different countries of the world, even on the continent of Antarctica!

I next came across David in Hua Hin, Thailand, at the Overseas Missionary Fellowship (OMF) retreat centre, in reality a very nice beachside hotel. I was on retreat prior to ordination and as I had three months to spare before starting my curacy I had gone visiting friends in the Far East. As I was to be the only one to be ordained at Michaelmas (end of September), I had managed to persuade the bishop that this was a suitable place to take myself off to "on retreat". My retreat consisted of listening to David's teaching on cassette tapes as he was very popular with the OMF workers there on R&R (rest and recuperation).

I didn't actually meet David and Enid until Cathy and I arrived in Basingstoke in October 1986. I was a very early recipient of his bountiful correspondence and we would meet up often to chat about theology, biblical interpretation and the church, both local and international.

Many of us will have enjoyed hearing David trying out his *Unlocking the Bible* talks with us in the late 1980s and early 1990s in our Lent series. I certainly improved my own understanding of some of the Old Testament prophets.

When we were doing a sermon series on The Ten Commandments and I was due to do the fourth, I went to my filing cabinet and pulled out what resources I had. Included amongst them was an article from *Crusade magazine* written years before by David. As I read it, I thought, "Well, that's what I'd say." So, the obvious thing to do was to ask David to do the talk. The article was about 2,500 words, which amounts to 25 minutes speaking, so it should have fitted into the evening service very nicely, or so I thought. But I had forgotten that David had once said to me that he couldn't really speak for less than an hour! Although David paid very close attention to his watch so as to start on time, the evening service finished somewhere around 9pm! We were edified, even though youth group never met that evening. The middle of the week, where he could have had two 45-minute talks would have worked much better.

One year, David and I were both invited to Spring Harvest, David as a main stage speaker and, me as a main seminar speaker. The theme of the week was on where evangelicals disagreed. I forget the precise make-up of the list, but David and I disagreed on most of them, starting with the age of candidates for baptism and ending with what the word "millennium" should have as a prefix! All of the issues were important but none fundamental to our both being Christians.

At the briefing for us speakers, a month or so before the event, we were both enjoying a refreshment break when Nicky Gumbel of HTB and Alpha fame came over to introduce himself to the great man (David, not me!). While chatting he found out where David was now living. David then wandered off and Nicky Gumbel was left to talk to me. He asked me where I was from. I said, "Basingstoke," and he asked, "Oh, do you go to David's church?" "No, I said, matter-of-factly, "he goes to mine." Well, I had never seen a paradigm shift expressed so facially before. His brain was in overdrive: "Who is this bloke? I don't know him, and David Pawson goes to his church." I could feel my perceived status as bagman rising to new heights beyond what I deserved.

In fact, David was kind enough to dedicate his book, *Once saved always saved?* (A question to which he thought the answer was, "No.") "to some brothers who take a 'Calvinist' position on the issue yet have been big enough to open their pulpits and platforms to me". He bracketed me with some rather illustrious company!

David had something of the "little boy" about him in his fresh enthusiasm towards a wide range of interests. He had an impressive train set in his garden shed at his home on the Aldermaston Road and a pond with exotic ducks from around the world and a black swan. He restored a Morris Minor convertible, which he enjoyed driving around the lanes of north Hampshire when the weather was hot. At Oak Lodge Nursing Home, in what was to be the last year of his life, he loved showing pictures of a car that his son Richard had restored from a rusted shell. The British Royal Family had once owned the car in the 1930s.

He was also something of an armchair architect. He had been very hands-on in the design of Millmead, the church in Guildford of which he was the pastor, and had learnt a very great deal from its architect.

"Why is it easier for us to focus on a speaker in an auditorium when there is something solid within 10 feet of their back?"

"Why is a square the best shape to seat 500 people?"

Our auditorium came about as a result of my attending a funeral of a member's husband at St Joseph's Roman Catholic Church in South Ham. I took the basic idea of what I had seen to David and with a couple of tweaks from Millmead added for good measure, he drew the layout. His drawings made life very easy for our architect to work on. Actually, even the upholstered bench seating and the chairs were made by cabinetmaker David Titcombe to a design of David's.

David was born in 1930, like the late Michael Green. David, a Baptist evangelistic teacher and Michael, an Anglican teaching evangelist. I wonder whether they have met up yet in heaven and have started sorting out what they had both been right or wrong about, or whether that has all been subsumed in the glory of it all.

David, writing about the dying thief on the Cross, in his book, *The Road to Hell* wrote:

"The most significant word, however, is 'Today'. There will be no need for Jesus to search his memory to recall the thief, because their relationship, established in such unusual circumstances, would not be interrupted but enhanced by their imminent death. They would be together later that same day-free from their painful and humiliating situation. Jesus' promise surely implies that they would both be fully conscious and able to communicate with each other."

In his evangelistic book *Truth to Tell*, David wrote:

"Blessedness – heaven – is to be with him, and that is the destiny of the saints. Heaven is where Christ is. Indeed, it is where God himself is, filling it all. In heaven there is no need for a temple, a holy place. It is all holy. I believe it is a place – a city, if you like – of such splendour that the greatest splendours of the earth pall before it. And in that splendid city a place is prepared for each believer, a personal share in the glory of God."

We extend our sympathy to Enid and her family at her loss, which we know will only be temporary. In fact, speaking of Enid reminds me that David did realise how fortunate he was to have her as a life partner.

In his autobiography he mentions how he was speaking about *Leadership is Male* at a women's conference in Germany.

Afterwards, someone said to him: "We have heard the truth from you, but we have seen it in your wife."

A one-time Bishop of Edinburgh writing a review of his book, *Leadership is Male* wrote:

"In searching the scriptures, he can only find patriarchy

or male leadership as the model for relationship between the sexes, and he is absolutely right. That is what the Bible says, along with a lot of other stuff we have long since discarded. Mr Pawson's difficulty is tragic. He is a good and kindly man and a fine Christian leader, but he is absolutely hung up on a fundamentalist method of scriptural interpretation. It makes him consistent, or as consistent as scripture; but he believes in doing what he thinks the Bible tells him to do . . ."

That bishop, now thirty years later, describes himself as being an "after-religionist" with an "agnostic worldview".

David's reaction?

"I couldn't have put it better myself. Apart from his pejorative use of the term 'fundamentalist', he has accurately summed up my life and work".

David leaves behind a life-long devoted wife, Enid, son Richard, daughter Angie and grandchildren, Guy and Aruna, and Evie and Daniel. David and Enid's eldest child, a daughter, Deborah, died in 1984 and is survived by her daughter Rebecca.

May David rest in the peace of paradise with Christ and rise to life in the new heaven and the new earth.

5. DAVID PAWSON: AMONG THE CHURCHES IN BORNEO
TRIBUTE BY DR THOMAS CHUNG

Dr Thomas Chung is a Canadian and UK trained physician and was the former head of pathology services in Sarawak. He has lived and worked in Borneo for over 40 years and is widely regarded as one of the leading Bible teachers in Malaysia. He has preached in the revival heartlands of Borneo and is a regular speaker at conferences in Malaysia.

I first met David Pawson in the early 1970s. I was a medical student at the time and I was leading the Christian unions in the London medical schools. We had a student retreat one year in Guildford. A fellow medical student, Steven Dyer, whose father Cyril was an elder at Millmead, suggested we visited the church for the Sunday morning service. I heard David Pawson for the first time during that student retreat. I was later introduced to David by Dr Kim Tan on subsequent visits to Millmead. I was absolutely captivated by David's teaching and had the great joy of spending many weekends in Guildford and attending morning and evening services where he preached.

Over the years, I had the great privilege of being able to enjoy fellowship and to sit under his tutelage in my regular trips back to the UK. Dr Kim and I would drive down to spend the afternoon with him. He was incredibly generous and often poured out his heart on many and varied issues, some of which were later featured in the books he wrote. Much of what he shared shaped my thinking and I was able to impart these teachings to the tribal SIB (Sijil Injil Borneo) churches (formerly the Borneo Evangelical Movement) in Sarawak and Sabah as well as the Full Gospel Businessmen Fellowship (FGBF Malaysia) conferences and seminars. Enid always made sure that we stayed for tea before departing.

One of the most significant events in the life of the churches in Kuching and of the FGBF was in August 1995 when Kim brought David to do a five-day conference on "Handling the Word of God". Before the start of the first meeting, a secret police officer tried to stop the seminar, asking whether permits had been obtained for the gathering. Fortunately, one of the organisers, who was a huge man, confronted the police officer and told him to sit at the back and observe the proceedings. It helped that he was a Member of Parliament and a Member of the Sarawak Cabinet! The secret police officer left soon after we started worshipping the Lord Jesus. In the mornings of the conference, I remember David doing four talks on Expository Preaching, Prophetic Preaching, Sermon Preparation and Biblical Interpretation. Kim Tan followed up with five talks on Radical Church History in the afternoons and David ended each evening with six talks on Studying the Old and New Testament, the last a memorable talk on the book of Revelation. Needless to say, every session was packed and 25 years on, those who attended (many of whom are now pastors and church leaders) still recall those sessions as important events in their understanding of the Bible and of the Christian life. On the Sunday morning, we took David to attend a service in one of the SIB (tribal) churches. The worship was in the national language and David had tears in his eyes and said to me that he was deeply touched by the presence of the Lord among the folk who had experienced the Bario Revival in the 1970s.

Over the years, David's audio cassettes and *Unlocking the Bible* video series have been wonderfully used all over Malaysia, even in the jungles of Borneo, and news of his passing prompted messages of condolence from many SIB churches all over Sarawak and Sabah. His *Unlocking the Bible* as well as many of his audio sermons are widely used by the FES (Fellowship of Evangelical Students) in the colleges and universities all over Malaysia. Many pastors and Bible colleges use them too, especially as they can be downloaded over the Internet.

David was a giant and he has made a major contribution to the work of the gospel and of the kingdom of God not only in Malaysia but all over the world. His unique style of preaching, clarity of thought, understanding of spiritual truth, not to mention the fact that few can match his communication skills, only means that what he has left us as his legacy will continue to be a blessing to all who love the Lord and the Word.

". . . he died but through his faith, he is still speaking" (Heb 11:4)

6. DAVID PAWSON: HIS ONLINE MINISTRY
TRIBUTE BY STEVE DALLY

Steve Dally is a former marketing executive and a trustee of the David Pawson Teaching Trust, where he has been the ad hoc "general manager". He has been instrumental in managing the creation of the website for the free downloads of all David's teaching, managing the transcribing of David's audio tapes into books and translations of videos and books into other languages. With a network of helpers and volunteers, Steve has developed David's online ministry into what it is today. We owe him an enormous debt.

In 1982, I arrived in Guildford straight from university to start my working life as schoolmaster at the Royal Grammar School. David had long since left Millmead, which was then a very different place from the church David had built and led. A new pastor and a new ministry team had been established and a complete generation had been lost through a split in the church. I could not have foreseen the future that lay in front of me and the impact that David's ministry would have on my own life and millions of others who at that time, like me, had never heard of the name David Pawson.

Out of respect for his successor, David had decided not to leave his tape library with Millmead and had asked Jim Harris of Anchor Recordings whether Anchor would become a distributor for David. There is a long story to be told here, but I'll save that for another day. Suffice to say, when David felt the calling to approach Jim, Jim was already "waiting" for David's call. Through Jim and the team at Anchor, David's tape ministry was secured and Anchor would develop this by converting tapes to CDs and DVDs, then to MP3s and online downloads.

I attended Millmead for some two years before my career took me into industry and beyond – just long enough to be exposed to the legacy David had left in Guildford and long enough to meet my wife to be. At that time, I was a young Christian searching to understand more about the Holy Spirit. A mature Christian family who were not members of Millmead loaned me a series of tapes on prayer: Praying to the Father, Praying through the Son, and Praying in the Spirit. I remember more about these talks than a single sermon David's successor gave. That is not a reflection on David's successor but more on David's style and the simplicity of David's teachings. This series of messages had a massive impact on my life, firstly leading to me receiving the Holy Spirit but also creating in me a desire to learn more about the Bible. I left Guildford in 1984. Many years later, I received a call from a close friend in Guildford asking me whether I knew any Christian physiotherapists in Reading (where I live). David had suffered a stroke just days before he was scheduled to record *The Challenge of Islam*. I knew just the person and passed on David's home phone number with a request for a personal favour, i.e. to go to David and see if there was anything he could do to assist and help David to fulfil a very important recording engagement "next weekend". I had done my duty and passed on the request and then heard nothing more.

At that time, I was commuting into London each day. I would download one of David's talks on MP3 from Anchor to listen to on my way to and from work. Over the years, I had built up quite a collection of David's talks and with them came many questions, but I knew of no one from whom I could seek answers. I remember one Saturday driving through Slough frustrated at how many unanswered questions I had when a little voice said, "Why don't you ask David?" But I did not know David and I was sure he would be too busy to answer all of my questions. After all, he was an international celebrity and I did not know where he lived or how to contact him. The same voice spoke again: "Well you have his phone number!" and I remembered that I had kept his phone number from the time he needed a physiotherapist years before. So, with some hesitation, I called him. David picked up the phone and I sheepishly introduced myself. Very graciously David said, "Well, fire away and ask." So I did.

At the end of the call I asked David whether he had retired, because I never heard of him having any speaking engagements. David said, with sadness in his voice, that he was rarely asked to speak in the UK these days and that most of his engagements were overseas. There was a pause then, followed by, "It just happens that I am speaking tomorrow night in Southend-on-Sea." Now I had never been to Southend-on-Sea, but I knew roughly where it was and guessed it was a good three hours' drive. It was a Sunday evening and given that it was such a long distance and my routine was to get up at 6am for my commute to London, with Monday no exception, my initial thoughts were that I would have loved to go but maybe another time when he was speaking closer to home, when David said, "Are you thinking of going?" I then started to reason with him and asked him if he knew how far away it was. He responded by saying that he had been there once before. They had offered him an apartment to stay over, but if I was going . . . wait for it . . . would I give him a lift? I was still not convinced, so I clarified with him that if the event was not starting until 8pm and he did not start speaking until 8:30 to 9pm, there was no way I could get him home until past 1am, and then I would have to drive myself home. David responded, "That's okay. If you drive at least I will get home and sleep in my own bed." I do not know why I said it, but I immediately responded with "David, if you want a lift to Southend-on-Sea tomorrow evening, I'll take you!"

There are so many stories I could tell you about what happened at Southend-on-Sea. That journey with David changed the course of my life. Before we had got to the event that night our lives had come together. I dropped David off that night and all but forgot about him. We did not keep in touch. About 12 months later, I happened to be driving near Basingstoke when a road diversion took me to where I recalled David lived and I thought, "shall I drop in and see if he is in?" I knocked on the door. David answered, and with a smile said, "Come on in. We have just been talking about you." My guilty conscience started working overtime – what have I done! David offered me a seat, and Enid said (without asking), "I'll put the kettle on!" I thought, "Oh no, what's going to happen next?"

David was due to attend an event with Revelation TV that evening and Enid had told him he was too old to be driving into London late at night and he should find someone to drive him, but there was no one David could ask. Enid had said, "What about that Welsh guy who took you to Southend-on-Sea twelve months ago?" to which David had replied, "I don't have his phone number and I cannot even remember his name." At that very moment I turned up at the door! It was another one of those occasions when I just could not say no. During that journey David asked me to give up what I was doing and come and work for him! I had too many commitments to drop everything at that time, but I offered to help David. That was 2010, and whilst I continued to work, I stayed engaged with David and his ministry and became part of it and became his "driver", "video producer", "publisher" and "close friend".

One year later, we travelled together to IHOPKC in Kansas City. I had just published David's book on remarriage, a book which received much interest at IHOPKC. I will say no more, but I was asked that week what IHOPKC could do to assist David and his ministry.

Before we left that week, David had a website, fully loaded with all of his audio and video that he had at that time.

From that moment on, I agreed with David that time was short. Wherever we could, we should record every message David would give, whilst the Lord gave David the opportunity to speak. Much of his video was old and of poor quality. The race was on to build and update a video library to broadcast standard. We recorded 21 talks that week at IHOP.

Take-up of viewings of David's website started quite slowly. It took more than three years before we hit the one million viewings mark. YouTube had also taken off at that time and David did not have the profile of many global Christian preachers, except perhaps in Asia. In 2013, we launched David's official YouTube channel, which had the benefit that viewers could find David for the very first time through searches. Over the next three years we recorded many important teachings and also published more than 80 books. David found it quite difficult to grasp the scale of his global ministry. The number of people who listen to David's teachings each week is far more than he could ever have hoped standing in a pulpit as the pastor of a local church.

David continued to teach right up to his 90th birthday. On one occasion during these last recordings, David confessed that one big fear he had was that anyone hearing these recordings might say, "well, he is not as good as he used to be." The truth is that he was not as good as he used to be, but with the knowledge acquired from 70 years spent studying the Bible still at his fingertips an old and disabled David Pawson was more capable than most younger men in their prime. He was still inspiring and a role model that had stood the test of time.

David never fully grasped what COVID was all about, nor the concept of "lockdown", but during this time when he was often asked "Is this the end of the world?" he would teach Matthew 24, using Jesus' own words to preach the good news that Christ was coming back.

At the time of David's death, there were:
- 71k subscribers on YouTube
- 10.3m views on YouTube since 2013 and growing

The Top 10 videos watched:
- UtB OT overview
- His video promoting his book remarriage
- Book of Revelation (recorded in 2002)
- Believers in Hell (recorded in 2016)
- Understanding the Trinity (recorded in 2016)

35% of these programmes were viewed in the USA
11% UK
6.5% Australia, followed by South Africa, Singapore, Canada, Malaysia, India, New Zealand and the Philippines, in that order. 50% were viewing on a mobile phone - 7% and growing were viewing on smart TVs.

In the first 90 days of lockdown in the UK, there were 1.5m viewings on the David Pawson YouTube Channel

His ministry continues.

7. DAVID PAWSON: FRIEND OF OPWEKKING MINISTRIES
TRIBUTE BY HENK DIK

Pastor Henk Dik is a retired pastor in the Netherlands and a board member of the Opwekking Foundation (meaning Revival in English) since 1996. Opwekking is a well-known interdenominational organization in the Netherlands that organises the largest Christian conferences in the country.

Twenty years ago, we published the first copy of the many books David wrote. It was more than just a book from an author coming to our conference. It was the beginning of a long-term relationship and a friendship with Joop Gankema, the former director of Opwekking, and as a result of this, David became a regular speaker at our conferences and we published 15 of his books as well as *Unlocking the Bible*. The words on the back cover of that first book *Word and Spirit* describe the exact reason why Opwekking started publishing his books and why David often came to speak at our conference.

The books we published have been a blessing to many readers, especially to those that longed to grow in their Christian faith, and people from all the different denominations appreciated the way David shared his enormous knowledge of the scriptures.

Unlocking the Bible has been a bestseller from the beginning and it is considered to be a unique study book in our country and a great help for those who want to dig deeper into the Word. The book was first published in 2007 and we are now selling the eighth printing.

Preaching at the Conference

David was a regular speaker at our conference for a number of years, but in 2010 it was a privilege for me to be his translator. That year was a special one for our organization. It was the year that our organization celebrated its 50th anniversary and it was our 40th conference during the days of Pentecost.

There we both were, neatly dressed, wearing suits and ties, and that day David started his message with the following statement.

"Many years ago I asked the Lord to allow me to minister, to speak till my 80th birthday and this year this has come true and that is why I stand here. This day (24th of May) is also very special because on the 24th of May 1738 John Wesley got converted and he became one of the greatest evangelists England has ever known. More than 750,000 people came to know the Lord Jesus and one of them was my great-, great-, great-grandfather John Pawson and I am named after him: my full name is John David Pawson."

He continued by saying: "If this is my last message, then I want to speak about my Lord Jesus Christ and the theme of my message is 'The Uniqueness of Jesus'."

It was a wonderful sight when David preached in the tent with close to 10,000 people and thousands outside. There was a great hunger for the Word and people listened with deep respect. Among the audience were thousands of young people and this confirmed to me that the ministry of David reaches both young and old and that they are willing to listen to 45-60-minute sermons!

A real English gentleman and a dear brother

A very funny moment for me was during a seminar in 2014 when he was answering questions and I reminded him that we promised that he would sign the books that people had bought. Because of the noise David didn't understand me very well and said, "Do you want me to sing? Don't tell my wife." While working as a volunteer in the Garden Tomb in Jerusalem we met again and I know that he not only had a great love for Israel but was a regular speaker in great conferences in the land, including the Feast of Tabernacles.

The present director of Opwekking is Ruben Flach, who has been leading the growing ministry since 2015. Besides the publication of books by David and other authors, and materials for children, Opwekking has been a leading ministry in introducing new songs to the church in the Netherlands. The present songbook contains 831 songs. Opwekking is also the Dutch partner for Global Leadership Summits.

Most of all, Opwekking is known for its conference during the days of Pentecost. What started 50 years ago with a group of about 150 people from Pentecostal churches has grown into a massive event with 22,000 people camping at the special terrain we build every year, plus the more than 25,000 daily visitors from all over the country representing all the churches and denominations.

In the July/August 2020 edition of our magazine we informed our readers about David's passing away and we mentioned that David's books and messages have been and still are a great blessing to many readers and listeners. It was an honour for our organization to have these close ties with this dear brother. Thinking about the impact he made, I used these words: "...he is dead, he still speaks"... (Heb 11:4)

8. DAVID PAWSON: ONE OF THE GREATEST BIBLE TEACHERS OF HIS GENERATION
TRIBUTE BY SAM HAILES

Sam Hailes is editor of Premier Christianity – the UK's leading Christian magazine. Before joining Premier he worked as a freelance journalist and social media manager. He is married to Stacey, lives in London and is a keen traveller, reader and tweeter.

"I ask the reader to compare everything I say or write with what is written in the Bible and, if at any point a conflict is found, always to rely upon the clear teaching of scripture."

These are the words of David Pawson, a man who devoted his life to teaching the scriptures. He will be remembered not only for his truly remarkable preaching gift, but also his gentleness, humility, and insistence that any question worth asking can be answered by reading and understanding the Bible.

David studied theology at Cambridge University and served as a chaplain in the RAF in his early years, before following in his father's footsteps to become a Methodist minister. Over time, he became uncomfortable with the denomination's belief in infant baptism and left, finding a new home at Gold Hill Baptist Church in Buckinghamshire. Later, during the 1970s and 1980s, he pastored Guildford Baptist Church and cassette recordings of his sermons began to travel. Soon he was being invited to speak at significant Christian events and conferences in the UK and beyond.

Uncompromising

David Pawson was uncompromising, but not in a "bang your fist on the table" kind of way. His delivery was gentle, sometimes understated. He never ranted or raved. Unafraid to express emotion while in the pulpit, he was often moved to tears during his messages.

He was not afraid to buck the trend, or to adopt an unpopular position. If the Bible said it, David would teach it.

Like many of his books, the 1,300-page tome that is *Unlocking the Bible* began life as a preaching series, before being transcribed into written form. It was inspired by Pawson's belief that the Bible is designed to be studied "a book at a time", rather than "a verse at a time". Given its size and relatively low price, it is probably the best value Christian book on the market today.

Other notable works included *The Normal Christian Birth*, which argued that becoming a Christian involves far more than uttering the Sinner's Prayer – and *Once Saved Always Saved?* with the question mark indicating Pawson's belief that such a teaching is unbiblical.

His autobiography was entitled *Not as Bad as the Truth*. Rumours and lies had been spread about the Bible teacher and speaking engagements were cancelled. Pawson complained vehemently to his wife, and then to God about the situation. The Holy Spirit's reply was "David, the worst they can say about you is not as bad as the truth." He laughed. But the point was taken, with God adding, "I know the worst, but I still love you and will use you."

Anything Could Happen

In 2009, I emailed him to ask if he would speak at our university Christian Union (CU). I had not expected a reply. At best, I thought I might get a response saying he didn't have time (too busy addressing thousands around the world, to bother with 50 students). I was shocked when I received a handwritten letter in the post from the man himself, graciously accepting my invitation to speak.

I had arranged to meet David at the front of our university campus. It was imperative that I was on time. My generation is used to texting ahead to say "running ten minutes late", but David didn't own a mobile phone (or have access to an email account – hence the handwritten letter). I made sure I was there.

"You're not going to make me sign one of those statements of faith are you?" he asked, as I escorted him across campus.

I gulped.

UCCF policy was clear: every guest speaker had to sign the statement of faith before addressing a CU.

David continued: "Another CU I went to tried to make me sign one. I refused. I wasn't allowed to speak."

I never asked him to sign the statement. And I never told anyone until now. Am I sorry? I don't think so. I still remember the reaction of my student friends, who up until this point had never heard of David Pawson. Their mouths were open and their eyes wide as they lapped up his teaching, with many remarking to me afterwards, "Where did you find this guy, Sam?", "He's amazing", "That was incredible!", "What a legend!"

To this day, I don't know why David didn't want to sign a statement of faith (he was orthodox on all the important issues), but he might have disliked the principle. In his autobiography, he explained how he would never speak somewhere if he was told *what* to say, or if he was told *what not* to say. That was one of my favourite things about David Pawson. You never quite knew what he would say next! There is no doubt that this way of operating cost him at times (for instance, it has been reported that he caused such a stir at one major Christian event when he decided to tackle the subject of divorce that he was never invited back). But he was a man of principle and integrity. Who could argue with that?

David's positions on male headship, hell and the importance of modern-day Israel were controversial in many quarters. He was especially known for his teaching on the latter, but often remarked how there were two kinds of Christian who followed his teaching: those who loved what he said about Israel but ignored everything else, and those who loved most of his teaching, but just wished he would keep quiet about Israel.

Nothing was out of bounds or off limits for David (he even poured cold water on common interpretations on one of the Bible's most well-known verses, John 3:16). But that was what made him exciting to listen to.

At one event, a couple of Christian missionaries were being interviewed about their work overseas, working among the poor. Pawson was due to speak after them, but the interview overran significantly. The congregation were settling down for a very long evening. They were to be surprised. Upon taking the stage, David Pawson preached what is surely one of the shortest sermons ever recorded: "Ladies and gentlemen, our topic for this evening is covetousness. In the light of all we've heard tonight, how dare we covet? Let's pray."

He had a number of clever quips, which you would always laugh at, even if you had heard them a thousand times before. An itinerant speaker, he would often receive a warm welcome, with congregations erupting in applause as he was introduced and took to the stage. David would always respond with, "Well, after that introduction, I'm looking forward to hearing myself speak!"

A Legacy Which Lives On

I didn't agree with him on everything – I don't think many did. But that wasn't the point. His invitation for listeners to weigh his every word against scripture was what mattered. He truly was one of the greatest Bible teachers of his generation, and his ability to hold his audience's attention for long periods of time was unmatched. As our CEO Peter Kerridge remarked this morning, "David Pawson was the only Bible teacher who could make Leviticus sound interesting!"

Like all great communicators, David Pawson never wasted a word. His scripts were edited and honed, so that his preaching was always clear and concise. Every syllable was carefully measured. He communicated deep theological truth in a way that everyone could understand. I couldn't have been older than about 15 when I first watched him speak (on VHS video), yet I was gripped. We know it was said of Jesus that "the common people heard him gladly" (Mark 12:37); and the same should be said of David Pawson.

This article first appeared in Premier Christianity magazine on 22nd May 2020. For a free sample copy of the latest issue visit premierchristianity.com/freesample.

9. DAVID PAWSON: PREACHING TO THE WHOLE WORLD
TRIBUTE BY JIM HARRIS

Jim Harris was the person David Pawson entrusted to make his teaching ministry available to a global audience, initially with the cassette tapes, then VHS videos, MP3s and CDs. Without him and Anchor Recordings, we would not have had the Unlocking the Bible series recorded, first in analogue and then digitized. We owe him a huge debt for faithfully curating David's teaching library. He was a special friend to David.

It was in 1980 that we at Anchor Recordings were involved with the Nationwide Initiative for Evangelism conference in Nottingham. I remember so well walking back to our accommodation in the evening with David. It was then that he asked whether we would like to distribute his audio tapes.

Audio tapes had been regularly made of David's preaching whilst he was at Gold Hill and Millmead Baptist churches, so this involved us taking these from Millmead and incorporating them into our work in Ashford. The cassette ministry staff at Millmead were very good about all this and David was highly appreciative of their dedicated ministry for him.

Over many years we have loved working closely with David and Enid. David's preaching style never involved speaking *at* people but he always took you along with him in his biblical argument. His teaching in *The Normal Christian Birth*, for instance, led my wife and I to be baptised by immersion (in the cold sea off Dover!). This particular teaching led him into controversy, of course, but this was not uncommon in his ministry. This was true, for example in his book *Once Saved, Always Saved?* I always found it to be a moving experience to hear David praying – you felt drawn into God's presence. Also, when he read scripture, he brought it to life.

A large step, both for David and ourselves, was taken in 1989. This was to ask whether David would be prepared to preach especially for a video recording. It seems strange today, but 30 years ago video was not easy with analogue recording on tape and viewing on VHS cassettes. But we chose to hire the best available and arranged special one-day conferences at schools, church halls, and other places. They were all very well attended. David was excellent and I think thoroughly enjoyed it all. I remember before he began the first ever recording, he and Enid took me to a room and on the table was laid out his suit, a polo-neck jumper, a V-neck jumper and other items of clothing!" He said, "So what shall I wear?" On another occasion we were filming *The Uniqueness of Christ* in a large school hall and it was sweltering. David stoically preached in his suit with a fan blowing on his back and everyone eating ice cream!

In 1992, David was keen to begin an important series called *Unlocking the Bible*. He had always wanted to encourage people to study the scriptures for themselves and this series was to introduce the library of biblical books – who wrote them, to whom and why they were written at the time and what God is saying to us today. It was quite a task to undertake for him and us. We hired High Leigh Conference Centre for long weekends twice a year; David covered six or seven Bible books over the weekend and this continued for the next five years. Occasionally, of course, something would go wrong and David would patiently wait and then have to start again.

Those were always great times together and good fun, and there was always a waiting list. It was a huge job for David in terms of preparation and delivery but this particular series has proved extremely popular and helpful worldwide – we heard they were watching the series in one of the Antarctic bases!

Every Monday morning at 9am he was on the phone! Following a weekend talk he wanted to go over it again and frequently regretted points he had especially wanted to include. On one occasion he forgot to bring all his notes! Some years ago, two senior Christian preachers were at loggerheads about some issue and David was invited to get them together and act as mediator. He asked me to be with him for a little support. David took the argument seriously, of course, but the thing resulted in them directing their anger at him! Poor David! "Never again," he said.

The experience of being baptised in the Spirit had a huge impact on his life and led him to possess an emotional sensitivity to God and peoples' difficulties and questions. For instance, God was never "All-matey" but is Almighty and David always gave thoughtful and detailed replies to the many letters he received. His chief motive in all his work was to ensure that his readers would be able to meet the Lord and experience his wonderful love and mercy.

Anchor Recordings was and still is a business as well as a ministry. David was always aware of this and his attitude to money, I found, was realistic, generous and honouring to God. What a difference that makes. He had enough to be content and enough to give.

David's legacy will be a lasting one, I think, for hundreds of thousands of people worldwide (perhaps millions). As Paul says, "But the Lord stood at my side and gave me strength, so that through me the message might be fully proclaimed and all . . . might hear it".

10. DAVID PAWSON: MAN OF GOD
TRIBUTE BY MALCOLM HEDDING

Malcolm Hedding was the Executive Director of the International Christian Embassy Jerusalem from 2001 to 2011. An ordained minister of the Assemblies of God of Southern Africa, he is now an Associate Pastor of World Outreach Church in Murfreesboro, Tennessee. Malcolm holds a Bachelor of Theology degree, is married to Cheryl and has written 17 books on various theological themes.

"I have fought the good fight, I have finished the race, I have kept the faith." (2 Tim 4:7)

His Calling

David Pawson was a remarkable gift to the Body of Christ in that he was more than just an outstanding expositor of the Word of God. David was sent out worldwide by the Holy Spirit and as such was an apostle, but he was also a prophet. From time to time, and, indeed, not as frequently as some, he would make prophetic declarations and these all came to pass with the passage of time. Though let it be said that David never assumed titles and indeed did not approve of those who did. A title for him was a designation of service and not of status. He was simply David Pawson and nothing more. David knew his frailty and recognized that he owed his gifting to the grace of God brought to his heart and life by Christ, and also ministered to him by his dear wife, Enid. He always acknowledged that her love and support gave him strength and made him the man of God that he became. She was God's gift to him and has completed her assignment.

His Ministry

David was a fearless preacher and, though of small frame, he could "pack a punch" as he faithfully preached God's Word. He never shied away from the difficult passages of the Bible and in so doing upset many but brought correction and balance to their lives and to the Body of Christ. David fully recognized and appreciated the power of the written word and so he became a prolific writer and gave himself mostly in this regard to the exposition of the books of the Bible. His most well-known book is *Unlocking the Bible*, but in all he wrote over fifty books and certainly every Christian can profit greatly by them. In addition, he reached many people by the medium of television and today his broadcasts in this regard are seen in many countries of the world. In all respects he was quite formidable but those who knew him well found him to be a kind, loving and generous man. If David Pawson became your friend, then you had in him a friend for life, and this was the great privilege that I enjoyed.

His Friendship

I first met David in 1980 via a cartridge VHS video wherein he presented the case for supporting Israel from a biblical point of view. This video presentation lasted two hours but it was enthralling and kept one's attention, even though, as David always did, he stood still, as if glued to the floor behind the pulpit. (David greatly disapproved of preachers who roamed the platform from one side to the other.) The teaching he gave in this video had a huge impact on my life, and the congregation of which I was the minister at that time, in Durban, South Africa. The very next year, my wife Cheryl and I took a tour to Israel, which also involved participating in the annual Christian celebration of the Feast of Tabernacles sponsored by the International Christian

Embassy Jerusalem. Years later, I was to become the Executive Director of this organization, but in 1981 David was in all respects the keynote speaker at this event. Again, our lives were greatly touched by his profound ability to expound the Word of God. The same was true of the years following.

In 1983, I, together with another minister friend, visited the United Kingdom and, because we were scheduled to preach in a church in Basingstoke, we decided to contact David with a view to paying him a visit, as he lived just outside the city in a beautiful cottage, which he had named "Still Waters". To our surprise he welcomed us and, for me, this began a personal friendship that remained up until his death. We stayed in contact through the years, mostly via written correspondence and, as those who knew him well can also attest, I now have a file full of his amazing letters that were meticulously written in longhand. I shall always treasure them. These were always uplifting, but as David was wont to do, some of these delivered a stern rebuke to me! These were transforming because he made me think about what I was preaching and teaching. I am truly indebted to him, as are many other ministers. Indeed, David was never afraid to give correction when it was needed and, consequently a preacher friend of mine, who knew him well, once jokingly said, "When dealing with David Pawson, you have to put your armour on!"

His Devotion

In the year 2001, I took over the leadership of the International Christian Embassy Jerusalem and in February of that year the ministry launched another Christian Zionist Congress. David had fallen out with the previous leaders of the organization, by virtue of theological differences, and had thus not preached on its platform since 1985. As I opened this Congress with prayer and a word of welcome to the participants, I saw a "slight-of-build" figure standing to one side of the auditorium at the back. To my amazement, I finally recognized that it was indeed my friend David Pawson. Having stepped away from the platform, I went directly to him to greet him and thank him for coming. I had no idea that he would turn up and then, and most humbling of all, he told me that he had come incognito, and at his personal cost, just to demonstrate his love and support for me. This was truly the measure of the man.

From that day forward, David became the keynote speaker at every Feast of Tabernacles celebration in Jerusalem and from time to time we would meet up in the United Kingdom to speak together at conferences, in churches and in Bible studies. I well remember a time when he, speaking at the Feast in Jerusalem, asked the sound people to play an audio tape of a congregation in England singing in tongues. As three thousand people listened to this heavenly singing, suddenly it changed and became all the more glorious and beautiful because angels joined in as the worshippers gave glory to God. It was amazing and, as I looked up at David standing at the pulpit, I noted that he was totally enraptured and tears were pouring down his cheeks. Clearly, he knew God and longed to be with Him in heaven. This in itself was a powerful sermon.

His Hope

We remained in regular telephonic contact and I was always amused at his real sense of humour. On one occasion, as we were celebrating his birthday, he, with a shrewd smile, stated that he and Enid were deeply in love with the same man: himself! Of course, we all thought that he was referring to Jesus! He thoroughly enjoyed catching us out.

When he was first taken seriously ill some two years ago I got on a plane and flew over to the United Kingdom to see him. By this time he and Enid had left their cottage in the country and were living in a retirement home in the centre of Basingstoke. He talked openly about his medical challenges while acknowledging that these would lead him home to glory. At one point he looked at me and said, "Malcolm, I have no fear because I am safe in Christ." David Pawson lived the truth that he so boldly preached.

I am thankful for his life and work and, by the love and grace of God, I have been profoundly impacted by him. David Pawson's ministry will now live on and impact many more lives because he left a library of his many books and videos for all to enjoy and be uplifted and edified by. These can be retrieved at www.davidpawson.org.

The Servant of God has gone home and so may we all finish as he did. Thanks be to God for the life of David Pawson. We will meet again at the still and peaceful waters of heaven!

11. DAVID PAWSON: A GENTLE AND GENEROUS SPIRITUAL GIANT
TRIBUTE BY DR DANIEL HO

Dr Daniel Ho trained as an engineer in the UK and obtained his doctorate from Fuller Theological Seminary. He was the General Secretary of the National Evangelical Christian Fellowship (NECF Malaysia) and the founder pastor of Damansara Utama Methodist Church (DUMC), one of the largest churches in Malaysia. He is widely respected as one of the leaders of the churches in Malaysia. In his retirement, he is a regular conference speaker in Asia and Australia.

We all know David Pawson as an outstanding and clear teacher of God's Word and that he expounded scripture to the great benefit of God's people globally, especially his massive cassette tapes ministry – tapes that were widely circulated around the world. Indeed, he commanded a worldwide interest in the Word of God, especially the English-speaking world. The publication of *Unlocking the Bible* was the culmination of that magisterial effort in print besides his many other books.

He would pepper his sermons with some interesting personal anecdotes. I remember him once saying when he was preaching in a church in New Zealand and a senior lady came up to him at the end of the service. She said how appreciative she had been of his sermon tapes, which she had been listening to over the years. At the end of that delightful conversation David Pawson asked her, "So which one do you prefer? The sermon tapes or the person in real-life preaching?" She kindly but boldly said, "The sermon tapes, sir!" This was one of his many interesting cut-to-the-chase episodes in life.

The first time Pawson came to DUMC to preach was in June 1997. He must have wondered about stepping into this quaint semi-industrial building in Petaling Jaya and probably felt strange as well. As he sat there in my office just before the service started, he said to me, "I don't know why I am here." I told him, "We know why you are here: to bring a clear word of the Lord to all of us." Sure enough, he did. There were a few visitors who came that Sunday for his sermon and every one was obviously challenged and blessed. In fact, one visiting couple went on to worship with us in DUMC to this very day.

He was a quiet, simple and self-effacing person in my experience. One who had no desire to seek fame or fortune. He could have made a lot of money through his teaching tapes had he wanted to. Instead, he was a true gentle and generous spiritual giant in heart and in spirit. But whenever he came to preach the Word of God he thundered forth with clarity and authority. He would just stir in all of us a hunger, indeed a longing, to want to get into the Word of God ourselves. And coupled with his expositions to show us what he saw in those passages of scripture, it just drove us on in the study of God's Word.

He was not someone, as we all know, who was afraid to address sensitive subjects and court controversy in the process. He did it because he felt his points were important and that his views were scriptural. And he could come out very strong. To my mind, his wasn't a dogmatism that sought to promote strife and division. He was gracious and kind in the midst of differences and discordant views. One clear example was about women leadership in the church. While I agree with him that leadership is generally male in church, I would not put it as as definitively as he did.

A good example, he argued, was Deborah who was not, in his view, a leader but a judge in Israel. In his book *Leadership is Male,* commenting on Deborah in Judges 4:4, he wrote in the parentheses that the "NIV "led" (about Deborah) is not helpful" in his view. But what is the difference between a judge in Israel and a leader in Israel when all the judges in the book of Judges were clearly leaders in Israel? To my mind, therefore, his arguments were not persuasive and most biblical scholars would argue, and rightly so, that Deborah was a leader in Israel.

It is also often argued that women leadership in the Bible arose because of the failure of men or the hesitant response on the part of men like Barak (Judg 4:8). But this is not a cogent argument because, besides Deborah, there are clearly other women leaders in the Bible like Phoebe (Rom 16:1), Euodia and Syntyche who were part of the Apostle Paul's apostolic team (Phil 4:2, 3) and we also have Junia (feminine) and not Junias (masculine, as in Rom 16:7 in the NIV), a name which John Stott and other commentators have agreed should be feminine. Even in the case of Priscilla we find that her name always precedes that of her husband, Aquila (Acts 18:18, 26; Rom 16:3, 4). It is the normal pattern in scripture to put the leader's name first if a group is referred to, as in the case of Barnabas and Paul in Acts 13. Not long after, it became Paul and Barnabas to show to us who was the new leader now. But it also goes to show the outstanding example of Barnabas's leadership in his willingness to let Paul take the leading role from then onwards. And we all know that without Barnabas there would not have been the Apostle Paul surfacing in all probability.

Pawson came a second time to DUMC to preach in April 2009. This was when he was already close to 80 years old. As usual, he created much interest, with many visitors coming to hear a good exposition of scripture. He brought a great word to us for that Saturday evening service of ours.

At the end of the service, I gave him a little booklet which I had written for his thoughts and feedback. Within a week I received a personal handwritten letter from him. Like a typical fine British gentleman of the older generation, he wrote in his longhand carefully. That appeared to be his characteristic trade mark. It goes to show the care and respect he had for his correspondents and friends, whoever they may be.

The John Newton of old, composer of the well-loved hymn *Amazing Grace*, was another prolific letter writer in his 'neat, small handwriting' style following that of his mother. John Pollock, author of his biography entitled *Newton the Liberator*, noted about his letters: "He wrote from the heart and the letters reached the heart, for his own past and his learning, and his experience with souls, gave him profound insight into what he called 'the study of the human heart, with its workings and counterworkings, as it is differently affected in a state of nature and of grace'." Many of us know Newton went on to publish his voluminous letters, which became a great encouragement and blessing to many people in the United Kingdom then. It showed the heart of a pastor.

Although without the colourful past of Newton, the words above could equally be applied to Pawson with his wide experience of life and his vast knowledge of scripture. His words touched the heart. They showed the painstaking efforts Pawson would take in communicating. More than that, he would read through the book, manuscript or letter carefully before offering his thoughtful and often incisive response. I was blessed and was challenged by his letter to me.

In the later years of his life, he started to make a diligent study of Islam and to teach it. This was a further blessing to the body of Christ. One of the questions he was often asked was: "Is Allah in Islam the same God as the Christians'?" And Pawson's answer was a clear no and I agree with him.

A simple verse to prove this point is 1 John 2:22, which reads, "Who is the liar? It is the man who denies that Jesus is the Christ. Such a man is the Antichrist – he denies the Father and the Son." When Jesus is denied as the Christ, the Anointed One and Messiah, we have denied both the Father and the Son and therefore the God that Christians believe in.

Pawson went on to say that since "Allah" refers to a different God from that of the Christians, that word "Allah" should not be used by Christians to refer to our Yahweh God. Moreover, he said that Muslims also believed that this "Allah" specifically refers to the Muslim God and therefore non-Muslims should not use this word. He is quite right in saying the latter but this applies only in a few Muslim countries. In all the rest of the Muslim world there is, in fact, no issue at all about this word being used by both Muslims and Christians. This is where I want to respectfully say I differ with Pawson.

Ask any Arab Christian for the God they believe in and they will all undoubtedly say it is the word "Allah". And they do not confuse it with the Muslim "Allah" because some of the attributes of the God these Christians know are clearly different even though the same word may be used. So, although the word may be the same, the understanding is different. This is the biblical pattern, and it is also in line with Bible translation. Biblically, for example, when the Apostle John was trying to depict Jesus as the "Word" in John Chapter 1, he picked the word *logos,* which was a common Greek word in use then. He had no problem of depicting Jesus as the *Logos* but the Apostle John did two things. Firstly, he divested from that word *logos* the non-Christian meanings and then, secondly, he reinvested into that *logos* the biblical understanding of what that *logos* meant. So John took the first 18 verses in that first chapter to define for us carefully what that *Logos* was so that there was no confusion whatsoever between what was meant by ordinary Greek-speaking non-Christians when they talked about *logos* and the Christians speaking about their *Logos*. There are other examples in scripture, including the practice of baptism, which was not original to the Christian faith. We just divest and reinvest. So, it is very easy to resolve such confusion. I would say, "You explain to your own people what you mean by those words and phrases and we will likewise explain to ours what we mean." That settles the issue easily.

We see the same practice being used in the Chinese Bible. In one translation of the Chinese Bible, it uses the word 神 (pronounced *Shén*) for "God". But the same word is being used in Buddhist/Taoist temples and these precede the Christian faith, as we all know. Yet the Chinese Christians are not confused and do not see this as an issue. Why? It is again just a case of teaching and explaining to fellow Christian believers what we mean by the use of those words and phrases. That settles it. Those in certain quarters sometimes try to impose their will and even coerce others to refrain from using those words and phrases, unfortunately. Such actions, as we know, do not promote mutual respect and understanding or foster communal harmony.

This biblical pattern of using common day-to-day words and phrases is likewise being practised rightly in Bible translation. When Bible translators go into a new culture to try to translate the Bible into the language of the people they do not normally invent or coin new words or phrases for the Bible. They look for words and phrases that are already being used in that culture and then they do the biblical pattern of divesting the non-Christian meanings from that word and then reinvesting into it Christian meanings or understandings. To use a foreign language phrase like *Yesus Kristus* (which is Greek, as we all know) for "Jesus Christ" in the Indonesian Bible, in my view, is a mistake. It is importing a foreign language into the Malay-Indonesian Bible. But if the word *Isa*, which every Muslim or Indonesian would know stands for "Jesus", is used it connects right away with every Indonesian. Hence, Bible translators always seek to use the common language of the people, which is also the biblical pattern.

Whatever differences there may be, all these pale into insignificance compared to the huge insight, understanding and wisdom David Pawson offered to the body of Christ worldwide. We truly thank God for such a remarkable servant of the Lord that he has raised up in our generation. We are all truly blessed and enriched, and I count it an honour and a privilege to have known him.

12. DAVID PAWSON: BRILLIANT AND COMPLEX
TRIBUTE BY DR PHILIP LYN

Dr Philip Lyn studied medicine at Oxford University and biblical studies at All Nations. Along with his medical practice, he is also the founder and Senior Pastor of the Skyline SIB Church in Kota Kinabalu, Sabah. As a bi-vocational doctor-pastor, he is well known as a speaker in many countries. He is one of the leading church leaders in Malaysia.

I had heard of David Pawson long before I met him. People kept telling me that I simply *had* to listen to his tapes. I was at university and an ardent follower of Dr Martin Lloyd Jones and his inimitable style of expository preaching, where every sentence of the Word was chewed and ruminated over before moving to the next and where a proper exposition of a Pauline epistle should take at least several years to complete. When I eventually heard David on tape, I was aghast that anyone could gallop through a grand Pauline epistle or a Gospel in half a year! My prejudice made me an instant skeptic of the man; he simply had to be a shallow expositor or a half-baked preacher playing to the gallery. I didn't listen to him again for years, caught up in the busyness of medical school in England.

After completing my medical internship, while studying theology in seminary, I chanced upon his tapes again, enthusiastically promoted by some of my fellow students. This time, armed with a grand assortment of systematics, apologetics, hermeneutics and homiletics to boot, I waded into his sermons again with a myriad of axes to grind, listening intently to simply expose his skimpy preaching. My change of heart was as sudden as it was unexpected. After many days and with some reluctance, the simplicity and brilliance of his expositions dawned on me and eventually disarmed me.

I think it was his voice that soothed me long before I logged into the content. He had this unhurried, unruffled mellifluous timbre that calmed you even if you were in the most edgy of moods. No hype, no haranguing, no hectoring. Just a fluent, considered and finely balanced explication of the Bible passage under consideration without sidestepping all those awkward and difficult verses. It was perfect for the tape ministry. His accent, a hint of the Geordie blended with a touch of Cambridge lilt did him no harm. It was crisp enough to be universally attractive and understood without being overbearingly upmarket. I was hooked.

Just when I thought I might like to travel down to Guildford to listen to him on a Sunday, I was told he had taken a protracted sabbatical due to exhaustion. For a couple of years, I waited for news of his return to the pulpit while I was working in London, but the grapevine gave scant tidings of his movements or his progress. I eventually returned to Malaysia without ever meeting him, a cause of some regret. But some four years later, he came to our city to lead a citywide inter-church meeting. That was in 1988. I was assigned to a team to host him. That was when I first met David.

I remember a story David told me about the first time he went to Australia, how a lady came up to him at the end of one of his sessions and said, "Mr Pawson, I've been listening to your tapes for years and now I finally get to meet you!" "Well," said David, "now that you've met me what do you think?" She smiled and said, "I think I prefer the tapes!" David loved telling this story. For me, he had quite the opposite effect. While others found him intimidating (he could occasionally look quite severe with his glasses and beard), I found him fascinating. He was a unique mixture of brilliance, winsomeness and complexity all at the same time.

He could suddenly explode with the most brilliant of insights, then throw out the most outrageous of statements aimed to shock. I loved it! His intention was often to disturb the comfortable and to perturb the otherwise imperturbable. He loved jumping in sometimes where bishops and angels feared to tread. Issues like leadership gender, tithing, baptism of the Holy Spirit, the nation of Israel in the end times, the charismatic movement, the Toronto Blessing and biblical eschatology were all fair game for this Bible teacher, given his outstanding ability to encapsulate arguments and see the big picture. I didn't always agree with him but respected his views immensely. I remember having an animated discussion with him on tithing being a New Testament practice and saw his eyes roll up, either in sheer disappointment at the flimsiness of my arguments or exasperation at my untutored theology. I am grateful he overcame whatever he thought of me then, to still remain friendly and partial towards this unpromising young man.

He was one of the earliest evangelical and biblically-entrenched preachers of repute in the UK who came out openly in support of the charismatic movement in the seventies and eighties. I will always be thankful to him on that score. I believe David's teachings in this area helped the evangelical church move forward in embracing renewal and in allowing a greater fusion of Word and Spirit in its life. It also had a profound effect on the spiritual trajectory of my life. By the time I met him he told me he had seen every miracle in the New Testament, including coming across believers who had been resurrected in his travels in Africa. I was to experience something similar many years later when God miraculously brought my four-year-old daughter back from the dead after a tragedy.

His teaching on the priesthood of all believers rattled many in the established denomination at the time. I remember a bishop asking at one of our meetings if he was seeking to abolish the laity and make everyone a priest. No, he replied, his voice crackling with prophetic candour, he wasn't trying to abolish the laity. He was trying to abolish the clergy! He was such an atypical Reverend! Such forthright New Testament exposition didn't always sit well with the establishment and over time, those who loved his biblical teachings eventually fractionated into those who were "for" him and those who were "against" him. Everyone had something which they agreed or disagreed with David Pawson about! But I don't think they ever disrespected him. By this time his stature and impact on a whole generation of believers were well and truly established.

He sometimes moved in the spiritual gifts. On one occasion when we were sitting at the airport waiting for his flight to be called, he turned to my wife Nancy whom he had hardly spoken to in the whole time he had been with us and said: "The next time you sense any strong, inner prompting in your spirit, don't be afraid to speak out and release the word. Don't doubt yourself. It is the Lord. He has given you the gift of discernment." Then he turned away, lost in some quiet thought. We sat stunned, doused in the sacredness of that moment. I was about to ask him how he "knew" what he had said was from God but thought the better of it and kept my mouth shut. Nancy never forgot those parting words. It was a release valve for her to grow in her God-given gift, which she had despite her innate shyness, and blossom into the leader she is today.

I think one of the reasons why David and I got along quite well from the start was in part because I reminded him of two of his great Malaysian friends, Kim Tan and Thomas Chung, both of whom had been close to him at critical points in his life. All three of us had an education in Britain, spoke with hybrid English accents, loved the scriptures and were at ease with British culture. "Do you know Tom and Kim?" was among one of the earliest questions he asked me when we first met. "They are my friends," I said. Thomas was back in a different city in Malaysia while Kim had settled in the UK. "You remind me of them," he would say, as if that constituted some form of solace for him in the midst of an unfamiliar Asian culture. That was the common starting thread but it was a good one to begin with.

The next time we met again on his travels to Malaysia, it was some five years later. This time, Kim came with him and he was much more relaxed. He was now teaching on the Second Coming, having published his books on *The Normal Christian Birth* and another one on charismatic and evangelicals, both of which were extremely fresh and insightful. I told him they challenged me to rethink the basics of my faith. We had many meals together and I thought I knew him well enough on this occasion to trade jokes with him. He particularly loved an irreverent one about a rather insular English village pastor who found himself in knots over the usage of the word "but" and "butt" while preaching in the United States. I shan't repeat the pun here but he was so amused by it that he asked if I could tell it while making a guest appearance at his seminars the next time I visited the UK! I'm glad to say I never took him up on this.

The last time I met him, he was speaking to a group of men in Basingstoke and Kim and I had travelled to hear him at his special invitation. Over the years, he occasionally wrote to me in his beautifully crafted and expansive longhand. At the close of each year, a newsletter usually came with an added personal note at the end. It was always a welcome Pawson item, but because of my busy schedule and tardiness in replying, those notes too faded in time.

It was at this time that his video series on *Unlocking*

the Bible emerged and once again brought home to me his magisterial gift of making complicated things simple. He was a giant in the unique way he communicated biblical truths simply, crisply and with great insight. His non-threatening, rational yet passionate approach appealed to vast swathes of people across Asia. I owe him a great deal for the way I expound the scriptures today, and I know for a fact that he also impacted a whole generation of Bible teachers in the Asian cities and also many indigenous Christian leaders in the rainforests of East Malaysia.

His wit was perpetually dry. He once said to me, "Philip, there are two marks of ageing. One is forgetfulness. The other is er . . . er . . . er . . ." And we would have a good laugh. On that day, however he repeated the joke one too many times and I wondered whether this truism might already have a personal element to it. Kim ventured to him that the second sign of aging was probably repetition! David may have left us, but it bears repeating that many of us will never forget him. He was as brilliant as he was complex. He left an immense legacy to the Church and a warm and indelible impact on my life.

13. DAVID PAWSON: BIBLE TEACHER EXTRAORDINAIRE
TRIBUTE BY JUSTICE DR PHILIP PILLAI

Dr Philip Pillai retired as a Judge of the Supreme Court of Singapore in 2012. In a distinguished career, he was the Managing Partner at two of the largest law firms in Singapore. He also served on the board of a number of corporations, including the Monetary Authority of Singapore, Singapore Press Holdings, SMRT Corporation and the Inland Revenue Authority of Singapore. He has a doctorate from Harvard Law School and was awarded the Public Service Medal of Singapore in 2003.

The Landscape

An informed survey of what passes for the "Christian" landscape around the world today leads invariably to the observation that much of this terrain is characterized by swathes of human wisdom, syncretism and biblical illiteracy.

Instead of *Sola Scriptura*/Only Scripture and *Sola Ruach HaKodesh*/Only Holy Spirit, what we observed in this "Christian" landscape are syncretic mixtures of traditions and rituals which replace or contradict scripture; "another gospel" and fables meeting the demands of itching ears: confusion powered and amplified by easily accessible electronic media.

Much of the landscape is characterized by consumer Christianity and not Word and Spirit-disciplined disciples of Christ.

Into this mixed landscape the Lord raised David Pawson, to "teach the Word in season and out of season, to convince, rebuke and exhort" those who have ears to hear.

David: A Teacher for all Generations

What marks David out as an exceptional and anointed teacher of the Word in our age?

First he takes and presents the "whole counsel of God": He does not select scripture to support his conclusions, but he examines all scripture on the subject in order to reach biblically coherent and consistent conclusions that were often unpalatable to consumer and humanist "Christianity". It is the discipline and rigour of his comprehensive study and presentation of all scripture on the subject that set his teaching at a magisterial level, ensuring that it will endure for generations.

Second, there is David's writing and teaching style, clarity, precision and simplicity. He avoids religious and theological jargon and understates his sharp intellect and scholarship. In other words, he is only intent on communicating biblical truth and glorifying Christ, not himself.

Third, his teaching style was gentle yet uncompromising: you are welcome to challenge him, but make sure you have studied all the scripture on the subject before you do.

Fourth, David was unapologetic about God's irrevocable promises to the Jewish people and the nation of Israel: "Israel is My son, My firstborn."[1] "Israel My inheritance"[2] and His promises of bringing them back to the land and to Jerusalem and their salvation[3] are being fulfilled in our generation. As such, on the basis of the Word of God and God's faithfulness to His Word, he nails the errors of replacement theology as, indeed, those of cessationist theology.

It is a clarion call to repentance from error and to return to the biblical text and acknowledge that the God of the Bible reveals Himself not only as the God of Israel but also the God of every *ethnos* and nation[4], which are the inheritance of Christ Jesus, the Son of God.[5]

---

(1) Exodus 4:22; (2) Isaiah 19:25; (3) Ezekiel 36 and Romans 9–11; (4) Isaiah 19:25; (5) Psalm 2:8

David was invited to speak at Singapore's Cornerstone Community Church. That Sunday, the auditorium was packed with long queues of people lining up outside to enter. The Senior Pastor asked the young people to come to the front to sit on the floor to make room for those waiting outside.

David gave a most compelling account of the historical and spiritual reality and significance of the Resurrection of Christ. [*The Resurrection - David Pawson,* on YouTube].

As I was sitting up front I was able to watch the youngsters, who were right before me. They had their cell phones and iPads with them but not once were they distracted. They were rivetted and busy taking notes.

Afterwards, I mentioned to David that normally young people would be distracted by their electronic gadgets but this time he had their rapt attention. He then explained to me, "when I speak, I pitch my vocabulary to clear and simple English so that even a 12-year-old can understand, and they do."

As we transition into the last Great Global Revival and Harvest, whole new generations will require accelerated, systematic discipling in the Word and the Spirit, to proclaim the gospel of the kingdom of heaven, from the end of the earth back to Jerusalem. It was thus divinely timed that the Lord would raise and preserve the teachings of his Word and his truth through David for the coming generations.

The pinnacle of David's journey was to produce his seminal *Unlocking the Bible,* which provides a comprehensive, contextual and systematic introduction to every book of the Bible. This work is timely for the kingdom generations now emerging globally who have a hunger for a personal encounter with the Father, the Son and the Holy Spirit and to be discipled to maturity and into the fullness of the John 17 generation.

For these generations, not only is the *Unlocking the Bible* series available in print, but also on the easily accessible electronic media, including YouTube. Print and electronic translations in Mandarin (Traditional) and Bahasa Indonesia, electronic dubbing in Spanish are currently available. Work on a Mandarin (Simplified) translation is underway.

It is a reflection of divine wisdom that the life's work of a very English man would be used by the Lord to disciple the generations in Asia, Africa and the Middle East, let alone North and South America.

David the Man: Glimpses

I first learnt about David when I embarked on my own serious and systematic Bible study journey, through reading his writings and commentaries on different books of the Bible.

I later had the opportunity to host him twice in Singapore (where he would teach) and to facilitate his teaching visit to Jakarta. I also met him in his hometown, Guildford in England.

His masterful teaching on the Letter to the Romans was unforgettable. He started by providing the context and reason for Paul to write the book: that the church in Rome following the expulsion of the Jews had become a Gentile church and had become resistant to receiving returning Jewish believers to the fellowship.

David demonstrated that the Romans is not simply about sound doctrine. He showed how Romans 1–8 is the build-up to the climax of Romans 9–11 and that the veil of blindness over them is temporary and will be lifted in God's time. Again, this is something that is unfolding in our generation.

I encountered the man close up and discovered his passion not just for the Word of God but also the God of the Word. His patience and gentleness were manifest when things did not go as expected. He would retreat to his room, wait on the Lord and then return fully composed and ready to press on. Not a word of reproach.

He was sometimes overwhelmed by the extreme hospitality that was showered on him by his many hosts in Asia. It took him a little time to get comfortable with how elaborately his Asian hosts sought to honour him as a faithful servant of Christ.

While we grieve his passing, we rejoice that he is with his and our Lord, Christ Jesus. We look forward to meeting David again as we all meet in glory for eternity.

14. DAVID PAWSON: FRIEND OF AN INTERNATIONAL CHILDREN'S LEADER AND PUNK ROCKER
TRIBUTE BY REVD IAN SMALE (AKA ISHMAEL)

Ishmael (Revd Ian Smale) is a singer, songwriter and author with over 400 songs, 14 books and 35 recorded albums. He is an ordained Anglican minister, a member of the clergy at Chichester Cathedral and a former Christian punk rocker. He has spent 50 years in preaching, teaching, performing interactive evangelistic concerts and doing fun musical celebrations suitable for all ages that he calls "Praise Parties". A lot of these years have been spent specifically ministering to children and families.

A while ago, I popped in to see David at his care home and found him sitting at a long table with all the other residents. Each had a lump of dough in front of them, which they were all thoughtfully squeezing to try and form some sort of creative shape, I guessed. As I stood behind David, knowing that he was a man of many talents, it took seconds to realise that shaping dough was very obviously not one of them. In fact, unlike all those around him, David's dough never developed into anything more than a shapeless lump of dough!

I got myself a coffee and was soon joined by a relieved looking David. It seemed that my timely visit had rescued him from the "dough" torture. It was then he asked me for a favour.

David explained that when he eventually went to be with

his Lord, most people would only remember him as either the in-depth Bible teacher behind a lectern, the serious author, or a face and voice trying to communicate scripture through a recording.

He asked me if I could write a few things about the human side of David Pawson, "warts and all", so people could have some insight into him being a normal human being rather than just a serious theologian.

Of course I agreed, so here are just a few of my thoughts and memories of our times together.

We first met up in 1980 when David kindly agreed to write an endorsement on the cover of my rather controversial children's album that I had just recorded called *Land of hope and Glories*. So immediately I knew that David did not mind putting his name to controversy if he felt it was something that would be beneficial.

Even in those early days, people were treating David like a living legend, but I must admit having just left the Christian punk music circuit, I knew little of his teaching ministry, I just found him to be a good, well-educated honest friend.

I do remember a lady approaching him once whilst I was standing next to him asking if he was the Reverend David Pawson-Tapes. It was after that that David explained to me, giggling, that one of the things that he was most known for was his Bible teaching on tapes (cassettes) and this lady obviously thought that his name was David Pawson-Tapes!

We did some touring together and sometimes we went in his rather ancient open-top Morris Minor. David had a real love for "classic" vehicles, and one of his hobbies seemed to be collecting and revamping them.

David was a typical Geordie who did not suffer fools gladly. If he felt something strongly or believed it to be biblical, he would just say it bluntly. No flowery language, no gentle approach and sometimes, dare I say it, he left those he was talking to with little right of reply. But this was David. However, I have to say that he became far more gentle the older he got, which I think happens to most of us.

I remember him telling me that his *Leadership is Male* was his most talked about but least read book. That came as no surprise to me because whoever thought up the controversial title must have realised that making a statement like that would turn off loads of would-be readers.

If only the words in the title could have been adjusted slightly to *Is Leadership Male?* personally I think it would have sold far more as people would have wanted to seek out David's opinion.

Around the 1990s there came a time when the prophetic ministry was rampant and the charismatic movement seemed far keener to hear the words of a prophet than a Bible teacher. David was getting in "very hot water" as some were now looking to him more as a prophet than a Bible teacher.

Now I would never tell David what he should or shouldn't do but my advice to him was always to keep developing his anointed teaching ministry because prophets seemed two a penny at the time, but real Bible teachers were very rare.

Whenever I did anything alongside David, we both invariably ended the evening getting into trouble and losing a few friends, but we never seemed to mind. We felt that we were doing what God wanted us to do and stood by each other because we believed in each other and were good mates!

I liked to introduce David to new experiences. One day we pulled into a roadside "greasy Joes" transport café for breakfast. I made my way to the counter and joined the line of burly truckers waiting to order my bacon, sausage, egg, fried slice and mug of tea but David was nowhere to be seen. Eventually, I found him sitting politely at a dirty Formica-topped table wondering when the waitress would appear to take his order.

Another fun occasion was when I asked David to do a bit of drumming for me. It was so funny seeing him sitting (without his Bible) and surrounded by drums and cymbals, randomly hitting each in turn with no apparent sense of rhythm.

I could ramble on for hours about the fun we both had together but let me finish with this. David was the most knowledgeable and capable storyteller that I have ever met.

For instance, having a cup of tea in a café in Plymouth David whispered, "See that man over there? That's A A Milne's son Christopher Robin Milne, and then went on to tell me a bit about the Milne family.

Whenever we sat together, he would tell me a story about something or someone and it was always fascinating.

What is also less well known about David was his interest in the spiritual lives of children and he was a great encourager in my ministry to them.

So to sum up, David will always be famous in the Christian world as one of the most respected Bible teachers of our day, but to me he will always be remembered as a very good friend and a person who was full of fun!

15. DAVID PAWSON: MENTOR VIA PHONE
TRIBUTE BY JOHN SPALL

John Spall is a long-time friend of David Pawson. Based in Australia, he pastored a number of churches in Brisbane over a period of 28 years, serving as Area Superintendent for 12 years. He served as the Chairman of the Africa Inland Mission for 25 years and was a board member of the Vanuatu Baptist Churches for 40 years. He took over the full-time role of the David Pawson Ministry, Australia in 1998.

My first knowledge of David Pawson and his teaching came way back in 1971 when I heard one of his tapes in Uganda where I was visiting missionaries on behalf of Africa Inland Mission. I didn't know it then, but what a date with destiny it was. Dr Don Lloyd, an Australian eye surgeon based in England, was a member of David's church and regularly travelled throughout Africa visiting mission hospitals. He would carry David's cassette tapes to distribute as he flew from place to place, including the mud hospital where my sister and brother-in-law were medical missionaries. By the way, in one of David's messages he mentions Don visiting the Pawsons and noticing something wrong with Enid's eye. He went straight to the Pawsons' telephone to arrange medical help and her eye (and possibly her life) was saved as a result.

Back in Australia, I contacted England to purchase more tapes and was told there was an Australian, Peter Bettson, who had just begun distributing them. Peter ran a large car auction business and had about seven older women who used one of his offices to handwrite labels and inserts for David's cassette tapes, which were mailed out to people all over Australia. Back then, there were probably only about 200 messages available. Peter became my best friend and over the next 40 years or so we worked together to promote David Pawson's insightful, balanced Bible teaching in many places. In 1974, personal computers became available and I had the privilege with a friend of devising a computer program allowing the cassette labels to be printed on the old tractor-fed printer. I approached the Avery label company but they had no cassette labels available at that time. We had to order one million labels to cover their set-up costs. Eventually, tractor-fed gave way to sheet-fed labels. People may have heard David refer to the honest car dealer in Australia. Well, that was Peter Bettson.

David visited Australia a number of times and asked me, as a pastor, to pray with those who came forward at his meetings because he didn't want people to treat him as a guru. Besides that, he always made room for the ministry and giftings of others as he did not see himself as primarily a prayer warrior. That reminds me of a time during a prayer meeting before David was to speak and someone in the prayer team prayed for souls to be won in the meeting to follow. David rebuked the man, asking him to withdraw that prayer as he was not an evangelist, but rather a Bible teacher. We gained further insight into the kind of man David Pawson was when he said that all the international speakers went to the capital cities so he wanted to speak in the country areas that missed out. This visit in 1998 happened to be his last in Australia and Jean and I drove him the thousands of kilometres between towns across four states. When he arrived from England, he said, "Well, now use me." And for the next month this humble man of God spoke up to four times a day – and we all know that David didn't give short messages – and then, because of news that a previous international speaker had taken millions of dollars out of the country in offerings – refused to take a cent for all of his hard work. As a matter of fact, David was very sensitive about money issues. He preferred to stay in homes when travelling on ministry rather than in five-star hotels, in stark contrast to some other ministries. Another noteworthy aspect of David's lifestyle was that, as he visited homes he usually had some tricks with him to open up conversation and fun with the children of the family. Our five children have fond memories of David's visits, particularly for this reason. He didn't want children to be left with the impression that the adults were all that mattered.

David was my personal mentor via phone calls and his recordings as well as during our travelling and holidays together. I owe him an extremely large debt. Thousands of people, including multitudes of pastors and leaders across the world, look upon David as their mentor as well, especially people in dry churches where they are not truly fed from the Word. May I mention just one testimony. One man told us that when he was freshly converted, someone had given him the video set *The Normal Christian Birth*. Once he began watching it, he was so fascinated that he watched the series in one day. Then he testified that he went to his tool box and removed tools which had not been returned to their owners, and went to his computer and removed copyright content that he hadn't paid for. He told us that up until he heard David he really didn't know how to live the Christian life. This same man asked our permission and that of Anchor Recordings to make copies of some of David's messages with subtitles in his native language and he sent copies at his expense to every pastor in his home country in Eastern Europe. From David Pawson Ministry Australia, thousands of sets of tapes were mailed to churches, Bible colleges and overseas missionaries without charge.

When we took over the Australian office full-time, because of our involvement in Christian radio around Australia we broke many of David's studies into two segments to make them a suitable length for radio and added an introduction and a sign-off by Jean and had them broadcast over a number of radio stations. When videos arrived, we did the same with them and put them on Internet TV that went across Australia, New Zealand, the Pacific Islands and Indonesia and this is on-going. We gained an insight into how deeply and widely David's teaching was influencing people's lives. We would receive phone calls and letters expressing the most profound appreciation of David's teaching and so many of them said that you could tell how genuine he was. And it was his integrity in all matters which impressed us as much as his teaching. David was also very human and some, including ourselves, found him very humorous and also a little brusque at times, but we could see that this was part of his utter honesty. One thing that was clear from personal conversations was that, despite his calling to give so much of his time to teaching, he had a deep love for his wife Enid and his family.

We felt prompted from the Lord – and had it confirmed by a prophetic word from a stranger – that we should travel around Australia in 2016/17 promoting David's teachings. We took copies of his booklet *The Amazing Story of Jesus* (paid for by somebody in England) and USB sticks with all of his audio material, giving them free of charge to pastors and leaders as we travelled the 28,000 kilometres in 13 months. We were greatly honoured when David asked my wife Jean and I to be his global ambassadors in 2018 as, at the age of 88, he realised his travelling days were over. Also, some years ago, David asked me to respond to many of the emails addressed to David on his behalf. This has led to the privilege of much ministry, though it is an onerous task to reply on behalf of a man like David. We have been amazed at the doors that the Lord has been opening in Asia since that time.

Only eternity will reveal the amazing harvest from David Pawson's selfless, fearless and God-honouring preaching.

16. DAVID PAWSON: AN ELDERLY ENGLISH GENTLEMAN
TRIBUTE BY STEVE & ELAINE SPILLMAN

Steve and Elaine Spillman are the Founders of True Potential, Inc. a US publishing and media company. True Potential publishes and distributes Christian books to a global market, representing more than 100 authors from North America, the U.K., Turkey, Australia, and New Zealand.

We first met David in Jerusalem during the 2007 International Christian Embassy Feast of Tabernacles celebration. As a publisher, I was there to promote a book. I considered this event "work" and had no intention of taking time off to attend any of the speaking events during the celebration. Finally, after repeated requests from our financial sponsor, my wife, Elaine and I took an hour "off" to attend one of the main speaking events. Reviewing the schedule, one session piqued my interest. A man was going to speak on the "end times and Israel", "Well," I thought, "this may be interesting."

From the balcony of a large hall, seating about 2,000 people, we witnessed a small, elderly English gentleman addressing an audience of zealous Zionists. I knew that many of those in attendance were American evangelicals, and I knew that the prevailing eschatological bent of evangelicals in the US was *not* what this man was teaching. I thought to myself, this guy is poking a hornet's nest. Then I thought, this guy is teaching what I believe the Bible tells us about the last days!

Before coming to Jerusalem, I had been struggling with a moral decision. Well-meaning friends had set up an introduction with a popular evangelical American author. Publishing this author's book would have been very good for business. But I didn't believe what this author wrote. It was popular, but, in my opinion, it wasn't biblical.

In listening to this little English gentleman stand before thousands and teach what is biblical but not necessarily popular, I found the courage to go home and publish what is biblical, even if it may not have been good for business, even if it wasn't popular. I felt that I had been put in this service for a reason and wanted to thank him personally for his teaching and inspiration.

On the last day of the Feast, as we walked out of the venue for lunch, I peeked through the open double doors of the main hall. The service was over, and the seats were empty except for a small crowd engaging or waiting to engage with the session's teacher, David Pawson. I told my wife and other companions to go ahead; I wanted to thank this man for his teaching and let him know it inspired me to go home to America and publish boldly.

I approached the group waiting to speak with Mr Pawson and took a seat several rows back to wait out the queue. Sitting in the row in front of me was a small English-looking elderly lady. As I waited, the possibility of a connection occurred to me. Small elderly English gentleman; small elderly English lady. Hmmm.

Knowing that the clock was still moving, but the queue wasn't, I took the chance and touched the lady in the row ahead on the shoulder. She turned, and I said, "You wouldn't be with Mr Pawson, would you?"

She said, "Yes, dear, I'm his wife." And so I met Enid Pawson.

I introduced myself and told her that I was an American

book publisher. I asked her to please thank her husband for me and tell him that his bold teaching here in Jerusalem had given me the courage to go home and publish the kind of books I knew God had for me to publish.

She replied, "No, dear, you tell him yourself." Then she got up from her chair and brought me to the head of the queue and said to her husband, "David, this young man has something to tell you." And so I met David Pawson.

I kept our exchange brief as I felt a bit embarrassed to be pulled to the head of the queue, and I felt sorry for David and Enid as they wouldn't be able to go to lunch until these people had had their turn with him.

I left the hall relieved that I had been able to dispatch my obligation to thank this man (and now, his wife) for the dose of courage his teaching had bestowed upon me. Thinking I was done with that, I rushed to join my wife and colleagues at a nearby hotel for lunch.

Thirty minutes later, seated for lunch in a large dining room, I looked up to see David and Enid Pawson coming our way. "What a coincidence," I thought. But it wasn't. They stopped at our table and asked to speak with me. David said, "I believe the Holy Spirit has told me that you are to publish my books in America."

That was my introduction to David Pawson and his lovely wife, Enid. David warned me that he didn't "do" email. Our relationship grew over the next several months, with him in England and me in the US, communicating via phone or fax; his faxes were handwritten. I had to make sure we still had a working fax machine!

As we began publishing his books in North America, we also discussed the possibility of David coming to America to teach. David has many friends and fans in the US, including Mike Bickle at the International House of Prayer in Kansas City, Missouri, and Pastor Allen Jackson of World Outreach

Church in Murfreesboro, Tennessee. David was able to come to speak in America several times over the next few years. Each time the crowds were hungry for his teaching, and he fed them, almost always to the point of exhaustion. He was very bold in his teaching but very humble regarding his own needs and position.

The Apostle Paul wrote to the Philippians that his life was being poured out as a drink offering on behalf of those he served. In watching David minister, I understood the meaning of Paul's statement.

David's race on earth is now run, but his ministry is far from over. Seeds are sown, they fall to the ground and die, and they produce a harvest. David's ministry continues to sow seed in books, in audio and video, and most importantly, in lives. Many thousands around the globe make up the harvest, and many of those become seed and continue the cycle.

Thank you, David for pouring yourself out on our behalf. Many of the seeds you planted are sprouting even now.

17. DAVID PAWSON: TEACHER OF THE CHINESE CHURCH
TRIBUTE BY TONY TSENG

Tony Tseng is a businessman and partner of a multinational corporation in Taiwan. He founded the Full Gospel Businessmen's Fellowship in Taiwan and served as the chairman for decades. He was the chairman of the deacon board in Bread of Life Church, Taipei, one of the megachurches in Taiwan for more than thirty years. Tony is the Founder Chairman and CEO of GOOD TV, the first Chinese Christian TV channel and network in the world. GOOD TV was established in 1998 with the vision of reaching the Chinese people worldwide with the Good News through TV channels and all digital devices. GOOD TV has been the key partner in translating and broadcasting David's teachings in Mandarin.

I sincerely pay tribute to David who was a man of God, follower of Jesus Christ, great Bible teacher, my dear friend and one who changed a lot of people's lives around the world.

I remember the first time I met David in the 1980s at a Christian conference in Singapore. When I listened to him, his anointed teaching immediately got my attention and attracted me deeply. His messages unlocked the Word of God and inspired my personal journey with the Lord so much that I fully understood the meaning of "the truth will set you free". I attended the conferences in Singapore several times and enjoyed his teachings a lot. After that, I didn't hear from him for a long time.

Many years passed and deep down in my heart I believed

that his greatly anointed Bible teaching would be exactly what the Chinese Christians needed. When GOOD TV was founded, I asked my colleagues to look for his teaching videos for broadcast. They spent some time searching for him until Ross Paterson showed up with David's teaching materials as he was given the task of distributing David's teaching, *Unlocking the Bible*, to the Chinese world. We started to translate and dub *Unlocking the Bible* into Mandarin. Originally, I hesitated a bit to air his programs on cable TV because the tapes were old, but his teaching was so anointed that whoever watched it in the process of reproduction was impressed and touched.

As soon as we aired his *Unlocking the Bible* on GOOD TV, we received enormous feedback from the audiences, especially from the believers in mainland China. Due to his popularity, many Christian websites in China posted his videos without our knowing. Audiences wrote to us that his teachings were so lively and vivid that they started to have the hunger for God's Word and began to read the Bible. We also received requests to make *Unlocking the Bible* into DVDs for people to study at home, cell groups, Sunday schools and churches. The DVD sets were widely distributed to the Chinese Christian world.

Having aired *Unlocking the Bible*, we asked for more of David's teaching series to broadcast, such as The Uniqueness of Christ, Israel in the New Testament, Charismatics & Evangelicals, Men for God, Final Facts, The Letters of Jesus to His Churches, The Epistle of James, The Letter to the Romans, etc. We put his video on all of our digital platforms: Internet website, mobile app, YouTube, and OTT. Among our fifteen YouTube channels, David's viewership has always been in the top three.

In 2010, I invited David to Taiwan for some video recording and holding a four-day Taipei Bible Conference. It was the first time after so many years that we had met face to face and had fellowship together. I showed David his Mandarin video and he laughed because he was speaking perfect Chinese. He was also surprised that through GOOD TV channels, his teachings were distributed to the Chinese world and he was recognized half a hemisphere away. I discovered that he had paid a price to follow Jesus and his life was not easy when we shared stories of what we had lost. He had lost his beloved daughter and I had lost my beloved late wife. A few years later, I went to London to visit him with my newly-wed wife and had a wonderful reunion. I showed him our new mobile app with his channel and videos on demand which people can watch and listen to whenever and wherever they are. He was so happy and glad to know that his teaching might be a timely help to people around the globe.

Many people's lives were changed because of David, not only through his teaching but also through his passion for Jesus. His teaching impacted the followers of Jesus and touched the unbelievers' hearts to lead them to Jesus Christ. One of the audience members gave a tribute to him after watching the series "Men for God": "I remembered when I had just got baptized, a friend of mine recommended David's Chinese YouTube channel. As I watched him, a warm, cute old English gentleman with grey hair, like Colonel Sanders speaking Mandarin, I was so impressed by his interpretation and insight into the Bible that. I couldn't stop tuning in to the channel. There was so much to learn from him for he was one of the most influential pastors in the world. His voice in the series 'Be ye holy, for I am holy' hovered in my head for a period of time and I am sure he is the man that he spoke about: 'Man for God'."

He has left us a great legacy in *Unlocking the Bible*, which displays his passion for Jesus. He lived out the Word of God and taught His Word well to the world. It was an honour to know him personally and bring his anointed teachings to the Chinese world. I was happy to be his friend and to partner with him to distribute his legacy and I believe that he still speaks through his teachings, in the form of videos, audio, books and in our remembrances. I spoke to him a few times on the phone this year and I intended to visit him in February or March but due to COVID-19 it was not possible, which is a real regret for me. I miss him very much as a great Bible teacher and also as my personal friend.

18. DAVID PAWSON: DE-GREECING THE CHURCH
TRIBUTE BY PETER TSUKAHIRA

Peter Tsukahira, co-founder/Pastor of Kehilat HaCarmel, an Israeli Messianic congregation, has lived on Mount Carmel for more than 30 years. He is a graduate of Christ for the Nations Institute in Dallas, Texas, and Tufts University in Massachusetts and holds a Master of Divinity degree. In 2000, he established the Mount Carmel School of Ministry offering intensive study tours for building bridges of relationship between modern Israel and the nations. Peter's international teaching ministry and his books have impacted many around the world with an understanding of God's heart and strategic purposes in the end times.

I first became aware of David Pawson in the 1970s when I was in seminary and someone gave me several of his cassette tapes. At that point, I began following the teaching of this English gentleman who explained so clearly how God has remained faithful to His promises for Israel. Before it was a popular subject, he was one of the few public voices who taught about the Hebraic roots of the Church and the Christian obligation to stand with God's purposes for modern Israel. It was David's resolutely biblical stance that impressed me and so many others around the world. He was not only an accurate interpreter of scripture but he also communicated the Bible's emphasis on drawing real-world wisdom from God's Word.

We had the opportunity to get to know each other some years later in the 1990s when he was visiting Israel regularly for the International Christian Embassy's Feast of Tabernacles celebration and conference. At that time, I was living in Israel but traveling extensively in Asia and hearing about him from churches and leaders there. He had quite a following in that part of the world! At the request of mutual friends, I organized a private teaching tour of Israel with David as the principal teacher.

We traveled in a van throughout the land, and the first thing I learned about being with David Pawson was his sense of humour. He was mentally sharp as a razor and a genuinely enjoyable person to be around. At one point, one of us said, "A joke from David every kilometre!" On Mount Carmel in northern Israel we looked across the Jezreel Valley to Mount Tabor and over the Kishon River below us. David taught from the book of Judges about Deborah and Barak's campaign against the Philistines that ended with the enemy commander, Sisera, seeking refuge in the tent of Jael, the Kenite woman. The scripture says that Jael killed him after lulling him to sleep by driving a tent peg through his head. But David, with his dry humour, told us that he "must have died of surprise" as Sisera could never have imagined something like that happening to him!

There are other memories from that teaching tour that should be mentioned. One was that David was recognized by other visitors to Israel wherever we went. We were a small group traveling without an entourage or film crew, but so often when we were at a biblical site, people would come up to David to greet him and thank him for his teaching. They would remind him of his visit to their church or conference somewhere in the world, perhaps years earlier, and whether he remembered or not, he was quietly gracious to all of them.

In preparation for that tour, I'll always remember something that reflected David's character. The host of the tour, a wealthy businessman, wanted David to fly first class from his home in the UK to Israel. He was very insistent and asked me to tell David about the flight arrangements. David was very polite but absolutely firm with me on the telephone. "I never fly first class," he said, "it's a waste of money!" He was consistent in his lifestyle choices and would not be convinced to change, even for a clearly more comfortable trip.

Theologically, David had the ability and inclination to stay close to what the Bible says. He could be counted on to honour the text above church doctrines and Christian traditions. He was also clear in communicating his positions and this sometimes did result in putting him in the midst of controversy. I, for one, especially appreciated his straightforward approach to the subject of God's ongoing faithfulness to His Word, including the promises to Israel. Although it meant standing against the tide of replacement theology, David was uncompromising in teaching the "plain sense", that is the clear message of the scriptures from both the Old and New Testaments.

As a teacher, David had a very wide knowledge of history and culture that he used to support and illustrate both his speaking and writing. Two of his lectures entitled "De-Greecing the Church" made a lasting impression on me. In them, he said, "Those who think the foundation of Western civilization is Judeo-Christian are mistaken. It is far more Greco-Roman." David went on to cite four examples of where ancient Greek influence dominates Western culture in obvious ways: architecture (public buildings look like Greek temples), politics (democracy), sport (Olympic Games), and entertainment (exaltation of leisure and human beauty). His focus, however, was on the influence of Greek thinking in the Church and how to remove it. He said,"The root of Christianity is in quite a different world from Greece. Your Bible tells you where our roots are. Our roots are in the Hebrew world—the Jewish world. That world was almost the opposite in every respect of ancient Greece. The Old Testament is totally Hebrew and was actually completed before the Greeks appeared on the scene."

These words coming from a man who grew up in the heart of Western culture reinforced in me the conviction that Christianity has arrived at a strategic turning point in our generation. Ours is a time of great restoration, a time to prepare the Bride of Christ for His future return. The restoration of the Jewish people to the land of Israel and the re-emergence of Messianic communities in Israel where *Yeshua* (Jesus) is being honoured as Messiah and King are prophetic fulfilments that point to the restoration of God's kingdom longed for by the disciples of Jesus (Acts 1:6). I thank David Pawson for being a Bible teacher who understood the Hebraic roots of our faith and one who wanted to turn the Church away from Athens and Rome and position it in the right direction toward Jerusalem.

There are so many things that could be said about David and it is an honour to write about my recollections of him and his impact on my teaching. What stands out in my mind about the times I was with him is that he made it clear that he was available to me as a friend in the Lord. That sense of personal friendship that he imparted to me was a powerful encouragement and made what he taught all the more significant. His life and ministry were well lived and stand as an outstanding example in our day when such things are rare. Along with thousands of others, I thank the Lord for having known David and for the seeds of biblical truth he sowed into my life. It was a privilege to witness the exemplary faith that he lived to the end of his days—leaving an eternal legacy to his dear wife, Enid, his family, and many friends.

19. DAVID PAWSON: AN APPRECIATION
TRIBUTE BY MIKE WAKELY

Mike Wakely has been part of the leadership at Operation Mobilisation (OM) since the 1970s. He and his wife Kerstin have been members and World Partners of Millmead since 1974. In 1989, they started OM's work in Pakistan, and that has coloured the rest of their lives. They founded Starfish Asia in 2003, a charity that serves deprived Christians in Pakistan mainly through education, and in 2019 handed leadership of the charity to a new CEO. They remain committed to Pakistan's Christians in a different role.

It was in about 1970 that I first heard the name David Pawson. I was in Calcutta, working on printing books and tracts for evangelistic teams with Operation Mobilisation in India. I can still picture where I was (close to the Salvation Army HQ) when I heard about the Israeli attacks on the Egyptian Air Force in the so-called War of Attrition. Shortly after that, someone (I cannot recall who) gave me a cassette with a message on Israel and the Six-Day War by a speaker named David Pawson. I was gripped.

In 1972, I returned to England to get married to Kerstin. I stayed with my mother in Guildford, and much to my delight I discovered that this same David Pawson was pastor of the Baptist Church in Commercial Road. We started to attend and began to discover the weekly feast of straightforward, accessible Bible teaching that fed our souls. The church was moving soon to a building under construction near the river at Millmead. I visited the site and met David in the construction company cabin. He gave me a tour and shared his vision for the new building and the future of Guildford Baptist Church (GBC).

To India and Back

We returned to India for a further two years, keeping in touch with many new friends in GBC. When the Indian Government decided we were no longer welcome, we came back to Guildford for a few months and committed ourselves to the church. David was in his teaching prime, taking us through books of the Bible, chapter by chapter, on Sunday mornings and evenings – and, as far as I remember, on Tuesdays also.

I think he took us through the Gospel of Mark and maybe John also. Tuesday evenings were different but no less inspiring and helpful. I clearly remember when he came to the arrest in the Garden and the part about the young man who was "wearing nothing but a linen garment" and following Jesus. We heard how when they seized the young man, he "fled naked, leaving his garment behind". (Mark 14:51–52) David brought the story to life. This was the young John Mark's way of saying: "I was there. I was there. I was involved too. And I will never forget that night, trying to find my way home without any clothes on."

That was David's gift and genius, and I cannot read that passage without being as moved as David was when he brought it to us so long ago. "I was there . . . " You can hear it for yourself if you Google David Pawson Mark 14. David's depth of contextual and cultural understanding – coupled with absolute conviction born of scholarship and clarity of exposition, and his unique insights into Bible truths – formed a style of Bible understanding and teaching that have moulded my own preaching, barely a shadow of JDP's, but still distinctive and rich in truth. David knew, as few other teachers know, how to bring the scriptures to life and make them speak to our own lives today. Happily, his legacy lives on.

David's writings – and messages in print – remain an invaluable and always devotional resource. One of his great gifts to the Church has been his mammoth summary introduction to the books of the Bible, both online and as a book, *Unlocking the Bible* – accessible scholarship. We attended one of the recorded sessions of this series some years ago – a great weekend feast. David had some distinctive emphases, often provocative and not universally accepted. But it was always hard to disagree biblically. I think of his *Leadership is Male*, his commitment to the Feast of Tabernacles, his suggestion that we will all be 33 years old in heaven, and so on. But always these distinctives were thought provoking and solidly grounded in biblical scholarship and understanding. We thank God for the way David's preaching matured, enriched and incentivised our approach to biblical truth.

David our Pastor

When my mother died in 1977 we were in Liberia in West Africa with the OM ship *Logos*. We flew home to an empty house. There was fruit in a bowl and food in the fridge but the one who bought it was gone to her reward in glory. It was a devastating time for me, as we made arrangements for the funeral, a memorial service and then clearing up the house, selling stuff and finding tenants. It left a gaping hole in my life with the knowledge that no one could ever quite fill it in the same way. David came to our home in St Catherine's. We sat by the window. I do not remember what we talked about, but I clearly remember his visit. As a pastor, he cared and his care was as powerful and meaningful for me, at that time of bleak sadness, as his teaching.

The Legacy

Before my mother died and we joined the *Logos* ship, we had led the work of OM in Nepal. Living with a team in Kathmandu, we introduced the Pawson teaching cassettes to the team and the many who passed through our team house. His cassettes went into India, and the testimonies to blessing received reach us still:

"We listened to so many of his teaching tapes. Definitely a gifted man who used his gift greatly to the glory of God." (Susan Dean, USA)

"Many years back you did introduce David to me. I have heard many of his messages through tapes and read his book. Believe it or not, right now in these days I am reading his book on Isaiah. And tonight I came to know that he finished his race and has gone to be with the Lord. I praise God for such a man." (Madhusudan Das, India)

"David Pawson was one of my favourite preachers / teachers in the mid-1970s. I have never met or heard him live, cassettes were good enough for me." (Anuj Patro, India)

"Great teacher, to us in one of the English-speaking men's OM teams in India. He was our great theological inspiration." (Høgni Johannesen, Faroe Islands)

"I was deeply impacted by the teaching of David Pawson and he visited the (OM ship) *Doulos* in Southampton. We give thanks for his life and ministry." (Mike Hey, Australia)

We returned after mother's funeral to our place on the OM ship *Logos*, and we took with us sets of David's teaching cassettes. We put them in the ship library. We promoted them to the ship community, and they were listened to by hundreds of people who passed through that ministry. When we left the *Logos*, we moved on to Pakistan and for the next ten years we led the OM work in Lahore. The library was full of JDP cassettes and, again, many people were touched and helped through them.

"I loved his emphasis on being people of the Word and the Spirit together." (Tariq Waris, Pakistan)

"He was a great preacher and teacher of God's Word. I remember listening to his series of tapes on Revelation." (Garry Goodall, UK team member)

"Great teacher indeed. I listen to him on YouTube." (Melvin Khan, Pakistan)

I last saw David in September 2019, in a wheelchair yet ever loyal to his Guildford friends, at the funeral of another great friend and former elder of the Baptist Church, who had led the youth work when we first attended in 1972. George Verwer, founder of OM, visited him a few weeks ago and wrote to me: "I just visited David Pawson, now 90 but of good mind . . . I gave him your regards . . . We had a good hour of fellowship."

When I heard that David's course was run and he had entered into his reward, I wrote this on my Facebook page:

"We received the news this week that David Pawson had gone to be with Jesus on Thursday, 21st May. Today I listened to an Easter message he gave in Guildford Baptist Church in the 1970s. Kerstin and I became members of GBC in 1974, and we are still members. We sat under David's teaching and were fed with what I still believe was some of the finest Bible expositions I have had the privilege to listen to, laying a foundation that has lasted a lifetime."

20. DAVID PAWSON: CRITIC OF PROSPERITY TEACHING
TRIBUTE BY KENNY WIRYA

Kenny Wirya is a businessman in Indonesia with numerous interests including shopping malls, plantations, manufacturing and real estate. Through his family foundation, he has sponsored the translation of a number of David Pawson's videos and books into Bahasa Indonesia including Unlocking the Bible. He is involved in a number of charities, including Indonesian Care and Lima Roti Dua Ikan.

My first encounter with David was during his first visit to Jakarta, back in August 2013. I was privileged to be able to spend a couple of days with David during his time in Jakarta. David was a truly humble man. Calm, soft-spoken and careful with his words in casual conversations.

During his visit, we hosted a dinner to launch *Unlocking the Bible*, where he held a Q&A session. There, I saw him address biblical questions in a respectful manner, yet with such clarity and precision. Despite having followed his teachings for almost five years, I did not know that David was such a well-known Bible-expositor. One of the best I ever came across. I have never met any other Bible teacher who has impacted millions of souls across nations, and yet was so humble in every way. He carried himself with integrity at all times and had no interest in personal gain or fame.

David was a Bible teacher who taught with integrity. His love for Jesus was very evident. And he lived what he preached. His teachings impacted me and my family in many ways. His teachings encouraged my family and me to continually pursue the truth by going back to the Bible.

David had a sharp and discerning way of explaining the background of the books in the Bible, providing an in-depth insight into why a book was written, its history, geography and culture. He drew and painted the scope of the Bible, making it so much more understandable and intriguing. He explained difficult topics in such an easy and simple manner, allowing many like myself to digest truth and implement it in our lives.

David made a promise to God, to always preach and teach according to this understanding of the book. He preached to please God and not men. He taught with clarity, precision and sharpness. He preached the truth and not what was pleasing to listeners, always keeping to the truth. At the end of every teaching, David always closed with a prayer of humility, asking God to blot out or remove anything that he had taught which did not accord with the Bible. David kept his promise to God until the end of his life on earth.

David taught many things. But in particular, I was greatly blessed by the teaching he delivered in Changi Cove, back in 2013 when David taught on the subject of grace and the biblical meaning and application for both Singapore and Indonesia. There I recognized that the biblical understanding of grace is far from the concept of cheap grace and the prosperity gospel that is widely taught. His teaching challenged me and helped me break away from the "soft" theology and teaching that I had been taught. It convicted me to grow my faith through biblical reading and learning. I desire many more to also grow in maturity in their spiritual journey by studying the Bible themselves. This motivated us to translate David's teachings into Bahasa Indonesia.

David's teachings remained consistent with the Bible, centering on the true gospel of Christ, which is a vital need in our pervasive culture of prosperity teaching and poor church governance. This need also led to the call for me to make his resources available to Indonesian churches in the hope of sharing biblical truth to encourage churches to introduce proper financial governance and biblical discipleship. These resources will also shepherd Christians into personal encounters with the Word.

David's teachings have restored and strengthened my faith, anchoring it in the Bible as I have become empowered by the Holy Spirit to become a more mature follower of Christ. I have been very blessed by his teachings, and I desire to make his resources available to many more. I am committed to giving the churches in Indonesia access to David's teachings. This eventually led to the work of translating David's *Unlocking the Bible* series into Bahasa Indonesia which took almost four years to complete. Since then, I have introduced David Pawson's teaching to more than 350 churches and marketplace leaders, and over 500 Christians through gatherings over the past six years.

I am personally indebted to David who was a great, gifted and humble teacher. And I am grateful to God for the opportunity to have known David in person, through Dr Kim Tan, my brother and mentor.

21. DAVID PAWSON: IN DEMOCRATIC REPUBLIC OF CONGO
TRIBUTE BY DR PHILIP WOOD

Doctors Philip and Nancy Wood are lifelong members and World Partners of Millmead Church. They served on the board of WEC International for 10 years. They spent 40 years serving the people of war-torn Africa, practising surgery and medicine. Their lifelong work included teaching and training thousands of nurses and doctors in the DR Congo. During their time in Africa, they were evacuated three times because of civil wars in the DR Congo and Liberia. In their retirement, they visit the D R Congo for three months a year and remain involved in the specialist training of national Christian doctors. In Praise of Simplicity is their biography.

My family moved to Guildford just before the Pawsons arrived at Guildford Baptist Church. I was studying in London at the time and remember going down to Commercial Road most weekends between Christmas and Easter in 1968 to hear David preach through Luke's Gospel. It must be one of the first times I have attended a Maundy Thursday service. David took us through the events of the upper room and the Gospel of Luke has been my favourite book of the Bible ever since.

   A year before we got married, Nancy and I were attending Millmead as David was preaching from 1 Corinthians 7. As was usual in his preaching, he gave several ways in which this passage (that suggests that unmarried women should stay single) could be interpreted, and he left us to think through our individual positions. Later when married and receiving four months of orientation at Bulstrode, WEC International's property in Buckinghamshire, we were again able to come down every weekend to enjoy David's teaching on Ephesians.

When we left for Congo (Zaire, as it was then), the church gave us a farewell and David preached from Acts 13. The church decided to support us regularly and has done so ever since. We were touched when a neighbourhood group quite spontaneously wrote to say they were concerned that after five years of marriage we had not started a family, and they were praying that we would. We were a little surprised as well but were overjoyed to discover that Nancy was expecting just days after receiving this promise of prayer.

As well as prayer and financial support, the church started sending us weekly cassette tapes of David's Bible teaching and we quickly built up a large library.

We shared these tapes with many of the 50 other missionaries on our station and we soon had quite a lending library going. The tapes arrived by post but to a mail box in Nairobi and were then carried by the Missionary Aviation Fellowship (MAF Nairobi) to Nyankunde. At that time Idi Amin was in power in Uganda and we steered clear, although now we come and go through Uganda all the time. I have no idea how he got to hear of it but we soon had a Catholic priest 500 km away who was regularly asking for tapes. After a number of Africa Inland missionaries had been blessed by the tapes they decided to invite David to be their conference speaker in 1977. He came and gave a week-long series of talks up at Rethy Academy, a boarding school for children of missionaries in the north-east of the country. This must have been a time when the President of the country (President Mobutu) was feeling a little insecure, and it was indicated that a Congolese security agent had to be present at every meeting to hear what this foreigner was proposing. The agent sat in the back row of chairs and had a simultaneous translation from one of the missionaries. He expressed that there was no difficulty with the talks, although I never did hear what he thought. I'm sure he was challenged and blessed. One missionary and his adolescent son found their lives transformed at that conference, and the son, now grown up, is investing heavily in an orphanage in the city of Bunia. David then went from NE Congo down to the capital to meet some missionaries of the Grenfel family who were distant relatives.

In David's autobiography, he mentions going for a long walk around Nyankunde (NE Congo) with a "somewhat athletic" missionary member of his congregation. That was me. He mentions that he went to his doctor when he got back because of an irritation in his groin and he was afraid he had caught some disease in Congo but his doctor was able to diagnose that it was irritation from the walk due to tight-fitting underclothes! My son Tim was amazed that David would mention this incident in his book – but he did. But that was David. He wasn't prudish and could see the funny side of the incident.

The following year, I drove a new Land Rover down to Congo across the Sahara, for use in our medical work. We were all set to go when we had a letter from our insurance agent to say they had miscalculated our premium and they needed a further £296. All well and good, but we did not have that amount in our bank account. David had arranged a farewell for us outside the church after the Sunday morning service and when he heard of our need he asked folk "to stuff my pockets" as they left the building. When we counted what David had been given it came to exactly £296!

There was one other blessing from that farewell. Harold Wakeford, a member of the church who had his own

Land Rover, noticed that our vehicle was not sitting straight. We had filled the back with medical equipment (courtesy of Mac Burton, another church member) and had broken a spring. Harold was able to arrange for us to have heavy duty springs fitted on Monday before we left on Tuesday.

I find it marvellous that David's teaching is still freely available on davidpawson.org. I listen to about one sermon a week and have many reasons to thank God for this wonderful mentor and guide.

22. DAVID PAWSON: A SPIRITUAL FATHER
TRIBUTE BY TAN SRI SIR FRANCIS YEOH

Tan Sri Sir Francis Yeoh is a leading businessman in Malaysia with interests in utilities, property, construction and hospitality. He has been honoured by the governments of Malaysia and the UK for his services and contributions. As well as being a friend of David Pawson, he has played a significant role in the growth of the Trust to promote David's teachings through the various digital platforms.

David Pawson was without question one of the best Bible teachers of our time. I consider it a most divine blessing that our paths crossed decades ago and I revered him and loved him as my spiritual father on this earth.

David taught as a true Bible-based teacher would, never teaching a text in the Bible out of context, which he lamented can often become an unwarranted pretext.

He was never seduced by the possibility of gaining popularity with audiences that he preached to or taught. He warned us of false prophets that God admonished through faithful prophets like Amos and Hosea. The false prophets of their time, like many prosperity gospel preachers today, only preached what the audience wanted to hear but not what God's heart and mind were on – subjects relevant to God's Church today.

He reminded us not to be too pally with God and in that process lose our reverence for Him. God's wrath against sinners and the justice that they face are matched by His mercy and love for them. We see His wisdom on the Cross.

David always wanted all his teachings to be given to all the nations free of charge. In this way, I was joyful to play a minuscule role in enabling this to happen. His teachings – especially the *Unlocking the Bible* Series – were translated into Mandarin and they were done so well by faithful Christian brothers like Tony Tseng, founder of Good TV in Taipei. Today, millions of Chinese are blessed by following David's teachings.

There was one moment that I shall always treasure. In 2003, we put on a Three Tenors Concert in Bath as a thanksgiving to our Lord Jesus for blessing us with the takeover of Wessex Water from the once mighty Enron, as we prevailed against Goliath-like utility company competitors. David Pawson was my guest of honour. I gave a speech thanking God for His blessings and also for the great servants of God like David Pawson. I received a handwritten letter from David a week later thanking me for honouring him, but he said I did not mention the name "Lord Jesus" even once, although I mentioned "God" so many times. David was absolutely right that I compromised by using the word "God" rather than "Lord Jesus" to be politically correct. I was warned by so many that England is no longer a lover of our Lord Jesus, and that even the word "God" will offend many.

From then on, I never failed to praise our Lord Jesus publicly and privately for all His blessings. Our Lord Jesus is truly glorious and worthy to be praised, without shame or compromise.

In David's last days I had the blessings to see him rather often and saw him celebrate his 90th birthday. He sent me a most touching message in a video.

I shall treasure this and many other moments when I was privileged to sit at his feet listening to his teachings on the

Bible. He taught me that Christians must live well and also die well. He went to glory peacefully.

Praise our Lord Jesus who sent this great teacher to us in a time like this. There is so much fog in the pulpit creating so much confusion in the pews. David brought much clarity through his teachings on the immutable character of our triune God. David reminded us that if we are to imitate our Lord Jesus, the Christ, we should be taught well and accurately the true character of Christ. He taught me that God is most glorified in us when we are most satisfied in Him.

We will all miss David, but we look forward to seeing him again in heaven and re-establishing our dear fellowship with our Lord Jesus – us and him together, in unbridled joy.

23. DAVID PAWSON: SCHOLAR & COMMUNICATOR
TRIBUTE BY DR KIM TAN

Founder Chairman of Springhill Management, a specialist fund manager in biotech and social impact investing. He is a partner in a number of social impact funds in Africa and Asia and a founding trustee of the David Pawson Teaching Trust.

From the various tributes, the reader will have seen how David impacted the contributors' lives in so many ways. Here I would like to recount some of my fondest memories of David.

David among Academics

David's ability to communicate God's Word is legendary. What is less well known is his ability to lecture to students and academics. On one occasion we invited David to speak at the University of Surrey on "Empiricism, Existentialism and Christianity". The largest lecture room was packed with about 400 students as well as the Vice-Chancellor. On arriving in the lecture room, David said, "Kim, I am in trouble. I've left my notes at home!" There wasn't time for him to go home to get his notes so he agreed to proceed anyway. Did it matter? Not one bit. For one and a half hours he captivated the audience with his arguments so that at the end the Vice-Chancellor said to me, "I wish all my lecturers had been here today just to learn how to teach like David." On another occasion, we invited David to a public debate at the university on "Christianity and Humanism", pitting him against the Professor of Humanities, a Jewish humanist. David held his own and we had a wonderful debate for two hours at the end of which the professor confessed that all parents who have children can't help but believe in original sin!

Is Leadership Male?

Along with divorce and remarriage, this has been one of David's most controversial teachings. But David was never a male chauvinist. Along with the hard time that I had persuading him to set up a trust to promote his teaching ministry, I had difficulties persuading him to write his autobiography. I believed it would be a great help to pastors and leaders. But each time the answer was "No". I didn't know it until his son Richard told me at David's 90th birthday party, that David had "promised" the family that he would not write an autobiography. I can still picture the day at his home when I asked him about it again. He then sheepishly said that I had to go and ask Enid to get her approval! With some trepidation I sauntered into the kitchen to explain why I thought David should write his autobiography and that David needed her approval, which she graciously gave. The next morning I had a phone call from David to tell me that God had shown him all the chapters for his autobiography in his sleep and that he had all the outlines for each chapter, exactly as we have it in his autobiography *Not as Bad as the Truth*. I think it was probably the fastest book to come off his pen.

The Encourager

When writing my first book on radical church history, I asked David for his critical comments. I remember driving to his home in some trepidation at what he might say. He had set such high standards in his speaking and writing and as a perfectionist, he didn't suffer fools easily! Over coffee, as graciously as he could, he told me that I had written the book for readers of *The Times* newspaper rather than the *Daily Mail*! In other words, it was too academic. He challenged me to write for a wider audience and suggested practical ways to make the book more readable. Instead of feeling crushed, I left feeling encouraged to re-work the book. That was David.

Integrity and Modesty

Those who know David and Enid will know about their integrity when it comes to money as well as their modest lifestyle. At least one of the suits he wore for the recording of *Unlocking the Bible* was bought in a charity shop and he was really pleased with his "bargain". The only time I had a telling-off from David was during our last trip together to Malaysia. He was already in his late 70s and we had a pretty hectic schedule lined up following the 12-hour flight. I wanted to fly him business class. I knew first class was a no-no with David. "Waste of money" as far as David was concerned. The only way I could do it was to say I would meet him at the airport with his ticket. I had a telling-off when he found out that I had bought a business class ticket for him but my usual economy ticket for myself. He wanted his ticket changed! That was David. He did confess to enjoying the business class treatment though.

Enduring Lessons

David taught us many things. But for me, the most important lesson was to "rightly handle the Word of God" through spending hours in the study. Good exposition came from careful exegesis and that required diligent study. He disliked the chapters and verses in the Bible as additions of the eleventh and thirteenth centuries by an English bishop and a French printer respectively. They are helpful for finding one's way around the Bible but make us prone to quote a verse out of context. "A text without a context becomes a pretext" was a favourite Pawsonism. When he spoke, he usually mentioned the book (like "Isaiah says . . ."), sometimes the chapter, but rarely the verse number. He wanted us to search the scriptures for ourselves and encouraged us to read whole sections rather than a few verses. Tied to this was his constant reminder to root the scripture in its Jewish culture and background. His messages on De-Greecing the Church were a call to understand the Bible and our faith through Jewish eyes.

Regrets

My biggest regret was and is that David did not record a series on Church history to complement his *Unlocking the Bible* series. He wanted to and had bought 30 books to get himself up to date. After a few months, I had a phone call from David to say that he didn't think he could record a church history video because the scholarship had become so voluminous in the last 30 years that he didn't think he could do it justice.

Another regret was that we didn't have David discipling more people on how to teach and preach. At Millmead I remember him taking a small group of young men with whom he shared how he prepared and how he would structure his messages. These practical lessons have stayed with me ever since. I wish more could have benefitted from his experience. I only remember organising one event with about 70 young aspiring Bible teachers and leaders. It was a full day's event and David took us through how he prepared. First by reading a whole chapter rather than a verse, as David was against using a text out of context, and then re-reading it until it was possible to sketch a skeleton outline of the passage. Then by putting flesh on the outline and thinking hard about topping and tailing it. One phrase he used repeatedly was that you must "add gravy to the meat," otherwise the meat will be too dry. He ended by giving us an example – a most unforgettable one-hour exposition on the Song of Songs. It was a privilege to have been there.

I also regret not factoring in more downtime on the preaching trips to the Far East. The reason was that David didn't want to be away from Enid for too long. Enid had difficulties with the long-haul flights because of her arthritis and David worried for her when he was travelling. So our trips tended to be pretty packed. But on one occasion we had a couple of days on the beautiful island of Pangkor Laut as guests of the Yeoh family. David entertained our boys and the Yeoh children with stories, jokes and magic tricks and we saw another side of David which we hadn't seen before. Precious memories.

24. DAVID PAWSON: OTHER TRIBUTES

We give thanks for the life and ministry of David Pawson. We are especially thankful that he gave us in OM a real welcome when others were keeping their distance. When he was the pastor in Guildford he opened the door for my own ministry and the church supported one of our long-term workers. We celebrate his Bible teaching and many OM leaders and others listened way back when they were on tapes that went around the world. The greatest thing I celebrate is that he persevered through many difficulties and challenges. Only heaven will tell the story.

GEORGE VERWER
(FOUNDER, OPERATION MOBILISATION)

We were sad to hear of the passing of David Pawson, whom I regard as one of the finest teachers of the Word of God in our generation. I enjoyed his teaching tremendously and he certainly lived to a ripe old age, full of days. I heard many of his sermons on cassette tapes, many of which I had transcribed, but all my interactions with him were brief.

YANG TUCK YOONG
(SENIOR PASTOR, CORNERSTONE COMMUNITY CHURCH, SINGAPORE)

David Pawson has always been a great friend of Revelation TV and we have enjoyed a warm relationship with him.

We had the pleasure of interviewing David in our very early days in our London studios, then he followed us to Surrey where we did a mini-series with him in our New Malden studios, and he even travelled to Spain to join us for a few days of programming in our Spanish studios! We have fond memories of him coming to speak to our group whilst we were on tour in Israel and we get a great response, even today, when we play that cherished recording from a Jerusalem hotel lounge many years ago.

Revelation TV viewers have grown to love and respect David as they have gotten to know him over the years through his twice-weekly broadcasts on Revelation TV and were quick to send us tributes of how David had impacted their lives over the years. Here is a very small sample of the many that were sent:

David Pawson was such a man of God and had an amazing gift of explaining theology in a simple, understandable way. The talk I found most helpful was the one on Arminianism versus Calvinism (faith versus good works). He managed to clarify my understanding by pointing to the Bible: "We must work out our own salvation with fear and trembling."
(Mina)

What an incredible blessing this man has been and will continue to be for many years to come. I have been involved in several home Bible study groups using David's teaching videos and have been so encouraged by the growth of each individual. Thank you, Revelation TV!
(Peter)

David Pawson was a great teacher. He always delivered his messages in a gentle but firm manner with great clarity, and they were always sound and profound, which made a high impact on me. Thank you, Revelation TV for airing such a great preacher.
(Aurita)

David Pawson was a wonderful, humble teacher who taught "with you" and not "at you". I really felt he was speaking to me personally as opposed to speaking to an audience. Softly spoken yet eloquent and with a twinkle in his eye, he often had a funny anecdote which would always hit the mark. We will miss him. What a lovely man and what a legacy he has left.
(Andrew)

Our team at Revelation TV are honoured to continue broadcasting David Pawson's teachings, even after his departure from this earth, in the same way that we continue to honour through our programming the late Derek Prince, Billy Graham and others, so that many more thousands will have the opportunity to learn from his great wisdom and understanding of God's Word.

We say well done, good and faithful servant. We shall look forward to having fellowship again in person when we meet him in eternity.

HOWARD AND LESLEY CONDER
(FOUNDERS OF REVELATION TV)

I would like to begin with how we first came to be made aware of David and his teachings. I was at the time a pastor of a church in Brisbane. One of the brethren gave me a gift of a cheap iPod which contained over 400 of David's messages. I put the iPod in my car for some weeks and then one Sunday as my wife and I headed to our usual church meeting at which I was to bring the sermon, I decided to see what was on the iPod. So we turned it on and listened to it for the forty-minute drive to the church. To my amazement, the one talk we listened to out of over four hundred was exactly the same subject and scriptures and almost word for word what I had been given by the Lord to preach on that afternoon. I then decided this was more than coincidence so I began to be drawn to listening to David more and more for several hours each day. The one thing that really stood out for me was that I couldn't stop saying to myself, "this is what the Bible says."

David has had such an impact on both my wife and me in how we read our Bibles. His teachings have helped us in developing our relationship with the Father, Son and Holy Spirit. We owe him a great debt of gratitude for the legacy that he has left not only in his books, his teachings and his DVDs but most of all, the legacy that he has left in the children of God, including our adult children and their children (the generations).

He even impacted our personal relationships that have been built with some of our closest and dearest friends John and Jean Spall who look after his ministry here in Australia.

More than all of this, I had the privilege of spending time with David. John and I had the honour of travelling with him through South Africa and I was blessed to see the living testimony of everything that he preached.

Thank you, David. You will be missed and loved by so many. You were truly one of God's great vessels of honour.

DAN MURPHY
(PASTOR, BRISBANE REVIVAL FELLOWSHIP)

POSTSCRIPT

So how do we remember David Pawson? Or more importantly, what would David want to be remembered for? Clearly, most people will remember David for his outstanding gift for Bible exposition. The enduring image is that of an unassuming English gentleman captivating his audience with this extraordinary ability to make difficult truths simple. He had a razor-sharp mind and an amazing grasp of the Bible from many hours spent in his study, but his intellect was never on show. He was always understated – a sign of his humility. In his communication he always chose Anglo-Saxon rather than Latin-derived words (sweat rather than perspiration!) so that "even the common people could understand him".

Some will remember his significant contribution to the renewal movement. He was one of the earliest evangelical pastors to come out in support of the nascent charismatic movement in the 70s and 80s and his emphasis on Word and Spirit helped the evangelical churches to embrace the renewal. Many who were initially skeptical about the renewal movement were drawn in by the balanced teaching provided by David.

Others will remember him for his boldness in teaching on controversial subjects. David's middle name could have been "Controversial". At one stage in the 80s and 90s, when David's name was mentioned, it was always qualified by "but he is quite controversial". But David never courted controversy for the sake of it. He taught what he believed was the truth and was willing to engage with issues where archbishops and archangels feared to tread. Issues like leadership gender, divorce and remarriage, baptism of the Spirit, tithing, the normal Christian birth, replacement theology, the de-Greecing of the Church, Israel and eschatology were not off limits for David. We did not always agree with him but he was always gracious and big-hearted enough to befriend even those who did not. As someone has remarked: "You're welcome to challenge him, but make sure you've studied the scriptures on the subject before you do!"

Those of us from Asia will remember David for how he impacted a whole generation of Bible teachers in the Asian cities and also many indigenous Christian leaders in the rainforests of East Malaysia. We owe him a debt of gratitude.

He will undoubtedly be remembered for his huge library of works, especially the *Unlocking the Bible* videos, audios and book. The videos were recorded over a 5-year period and represented a monumental commitment by David, Enid and Jim Harris and his team. The number of viewings of David's teachings via video streaming, audio, YouTube and satellite broadcast have far exceeded the expectations that we had when his trust was formed to promote his ministry.

I believe the best way to remember David is by making his library of teaching materials accessible to the next and successive generations. That is what he would have wanted. To do that, the trustees are engaged in upgrading his videos to make them more relevant to the modern viewer, translating his videos and books into other languages and making his teaching available through as many channels as possible. The whole purpose of the trust was to make David's exceptional expository teaching available to the Church after he had gone because there will always be a need for biblical exposition. Those of us who have been blessed and impacted by David can play our part in promoting his teaching to our networks. To see his teaching impacting successive generations would make David very happy indeed. That is the legacy he would have wanted. It would make the sacrifices that he, Enid and the family have made over many decades worthwhile. We will have to wait for heaven to reveal the full story of the impact of David's life and ministry.

ABOUT DAVID PAWSON

A speaker and author with uncompromising faithfulness to the Holy Scriptures, David brings clarity and a message of urgency to Christians to uncover hidden treasures in God's Word.

Born in England in 1930, David began his career with a degree in Agriculture from Durham University. When God intervened and called him to become a Minister, he completed an MA in Theology at Cambridge University and served as a Chaplain in the Royal Air Force for three years. He moved on to pastor several churches, including the Millmead Centre in Guildford, which became a model for many UK church leaders. In 1979, the Lord led him into an international ministry. His current itinerant ministry is predominantly to church leaders. David and his wife Enid currently reside in the county of Hampshire in the UK.

Over the years, he has written a large number of books, booklets, and daily reading notes. His extensive and very accessible overviews of the books of the Bible have been published and recorded in *Unlocking the Bible*. Millions of copies of his teachings have been distributed in more than 120 countries, providing a solid biblical foundation.

He is reputed to be the "most influential Western preacher in China" through the broadcast of his best-selling *Unlocking the Bible* series into every Chinese province by Good TV. In the UK, David's teachings are often broadcast on Revelation TV.

Countless believers worldwide have also benefited from his generous decision in 2011 to make available his extensive audio video teaching library free of charge at **www.davidpawson.org** and we have recently uploaded all of David's video to a dedicated channel on **www.youtube.com**

UNLOCKING THE BIBLE

A unique overview of both the Old and New Testaments, from internationally acclaimed evangelical speaker and author David Pawson. *Unlocking the Bible* opens up the Word of God in a fresh and powerful way. Avoiding the small detail of verse by verse studies, it sets out the epic story of God and his people in Israel. The culture, historical background and people are introduced and the teaching applied to the modern world. Eight volumes have been brought into one compact and easy to use guide to cover both the Old and New Testaments in one massive omnibus edition. *The Old Testament: The Maker's Instructions* (The five books of law); *A Land and A Kingdom* (Joshua, Judges, Ruth, 1&2 Samuel, 1&2 Kings); *Poems of Worship and Wisdom* (Psalms, Song of Solomon, Proverbs, Ecclesiastes, Job); *Decline and Fall of an Empire* (Isaiah, Jeremiah and other prophets); *The Struggle to Survive* (Chronicles and prophets of exile); *The New Testament: The Hinge of History* (Mathew, Mark, Luke, John and Acts); *The Thirteenth Apostle* (Paul and his letters); *Through Suffering to Glory* (Hebrews, the letters of James, Peter and Jude, the Book of Revelation). Already an international bestseller.

OTHER LANGUAGES

Unlocking the Bible is available in book, video and audio formats and has been translated into other languages.

WATCH DAVID'S INTRO
www.davidpawson.com/utbintro

WATCH
www.davidpawson.com/utbwatch

LISTEN
www.davidpawson.com/utblisten

PURCHASE THE BOOK
www.davidpawson.com/utbbuybook

PURCHASE THE EBOOK
www.davidpawson.com/utbbuykindle

PURCHASE THE DVD
www.davidpawson.com/utbbuydvd

PURCHASE USB
FLASH DRIVE INCLUDING:
- ALL VIDEO (MP4)
- ALL AUDIO TRACKS (MP3)
- CHARTS (PDF)

www.davidpawson.com/buyusb

THE EXPLAINING SERIES
BIBLICAL TRUTH SIMPLY EXPLAINED

If you have been blessed reading this book, we have more books available in David's Explaining Series. Please register to download for free by visiting **www.explainingbiblicaltruth.global**

Other booklets in the *Explaining* series include:
The Amazing Story of Jesus
The Resurrection: *The Heart of Christianity*
Studying the Bible
Being Anointed and Filled with the Holy Spirit
New Testament Baptism
How to study a book of the Bible: Jude
The Key Steps to Becoming a Christian
What the Bible says about Money
What the Bible says about Work
Grace – *Undeserved Favour, Irresistible Force or Unconditional Forgiveness?*
Eternally secure? – *What the Bible says about being saved*
De-Greecing the Church – The impact of Greek thinking on Christian beliefs
Three texts often taken out of context: *Expounding the truth and exposing error*
The Trinity
The Truth about Christmas

They will also be available to purchase as print copies from:
Amazon or **www.thebookdepository.com**

JESUS: THE SEVEN WONDERS OF HISTORY

This book is the result of a lifetime of telling 'the greatest story ever told' around the world. David re-told it to many hundreds of young people in Kansas City, USA, who heard it with uninhibited enthusiasm, 'tweeting' on the internet about 'this cute old English gentleman' even while he was speaking.

Taking the middle section of the Apostles' Creed as a framework, David explains the fundamental facts about Jesus on which the Christian faith is based in a fresh and stimulating way. Both old and new Christians will benefit from this 'back to basics' call and find themselves falling in love with their Lord all over again.

OTHER TEACHINGS
BY DAVID PAWSON

For the most up to date list of David's Books
go to: **www.davidpawsonbooks.com**

To purchase David's Teachings
go to: **www.davidpawson.com**

www.ingramcontent.com/pod-product-compliance
Lightning Source LLC
Chambersburg PA
CBHW071519080526
44588CB00011B/1486